THE *Fruit* OF THE SPIRIT IS . . . *Love*

THE *Fruit* OF THE SPIRIT IS . . . *Love*

A small group Bible study

Lynn Stanley

For the reader's convenience, the author cites verses from the King James *and* the New International Versions of the Bible. The translations appear side-by-side, with the NIV always appearing to the *left* of the KJV.

FOCUS PUBLISHING
502 Third Street N.W.
Bemidji, MN 56601

A small group Bible study

Lynn Stanley

ISBN 1-885904-45-2

Cover Design By
Barb Van Thomma

Printed in the United States of America

From the Author

The Holy Spirit of God is not an apparition; He is a real person, who dwells in the hearts of all who believe on the name of Jesus Christ (1 Corinthians 6:19), trust in Him as Savior (Ephesians 1:13), and follow the commandments of God (1 John 3:24). The author would be remiss in offering a study on the fruit of the Holy Spirit without first stressing the need for all who read it to be saved:

> ***...I tell you the truth, no one can see the kingdom of God unless he is born again. ...No one can enter the kingdom of God unless he is born of water and the Spirit.***
>
> **—John 3:3, 5 NIV**

> ***...“The word is near you; it is in your mouth and in your heart,” that is, the word of faith we are proclaiming: That if you confess with your mouth, “Jesus is Lord,” and believe in your heart that God raised him from the dead, you will be saved. For it is with your heart that you believe and are justified, and it is with your mouth that you confess and are saved.”*** **—Romans 10:8-10**

> ***And you also were included in Christ when you heard the word of truth, the gospel of your salvation. Having believed, you were marked in him with a seal, the promised Holy Spirit.***
>
> **—Ephesians 1:13**

All who desire to fully experience the supernatural power of God’s Holy Spirit, must first confess their sins, being fully repentant, and open to God’s intervention in their lives. Second, they must believe that Jesus Christ died for their sins, was buried, rose from the dead and lives today.

For Fred, Tracie and B.J.

"A happy family is but an earlier heaven."
—Sir John Bowring

Contents

love: 1 a (1) : strong affection of another arising out of kinship or personal ties **(2) :** attraction based on sexual desire: affection and tenderness felt by lovers **(3) :** affection based on admiration, benevolence, or common interests. **b :** an assurance of love **2 :** warm attachment, enthusiasm, or devotion **3 a :** the object of attachment, devotion, or admiration b : a beloved person: DARLING —often used as a term or endearment **4 a :** unselfish loyal and benevolent concern for the good of another **b :** a person's adoration of God **5 :** a god or personification of love

"I do not hide your righteousness in my heart; I speak of your faithfulness and salvation. I do not conceal your love and your truth from the great assembly."

Psalm 40:10-11

Chapter 1

God is Love

Whoever does not love does not know God, because God is love.

1 John 4:8 (NIV)

"God is Love. This is at once the most universally known and universally misunderstood attribute of all."

— H.L. Wilmington

For centuries men and women have attempted to typify God. Some describe the Almighty as "a spirit," while others claim He is simply a representation of goodness.

Visually, the ancient hieroglyphic for God was the figure of an eye upon a scepter, signifying that the Creator sees all and rules all. And throughout the ages, many artists have left their perceptions of the Almighty on canvas and paper.

However sincere the countless efforts to describe God, no mortal rendering—verbal or visual—can adequately define Him. Though he earnestly and continually tries, man's finite intellect and creativity will always limit his ability to perceive and describe the awesome and Almighty God Most High.

In trying to define God, many have also attempted to define love. Goethe wrote that we are shaped and fashioned by what we love. Balzac said that love is to the moral nature what the sun is to the earth, and Martin Luther taught that love is the image of God…the living essence of the divine nature. And presumably, no one has been more often quoted on the subject of love than the Apostle John, who said— simply—*God is love.*

With the exception of the contemplation of the One Who *is* Love, no topic has been more frequently defined or debated—no element of human nature more scrutinized—than the nature and essence of *love*. Love is an "emotion," a "response," a "reaction," an "opinion," and an "attitude." Most importantly, love is an "attribute" of the one who possesses it and an *action* of the one who rightly understands it.

Because *God is love*, one cannot understand love if one does not first have an accurate view of the One who *is* Love. To say that *God is love* is to claim that the two are indistinguishable; whatever authentic love is, God is. God is good, merciful, compassionate, faithful, protective…God's love seeks the best for others; *God never fails*. Likewise, whatever God is, genuine love is. Love is patient, kind, perfect, pure, just, self-sacrificing, forgiving, trustworthy, and true…*love never fails*.

Our perception of God will determine how we live and love. Those who view Jesus as Savior and Lord will presumably attempt to live life in His Spirit. Jesus came to demonstrate the love of His Father to the world; He was "love in the flesh" to people of every class, creed, and color. Jesus loved perfectly, profusely, and unconditionally. He loved the poor, the homely, the sick, and the sinner. He loved those who loved Him, and He loved those who hated Him. Jesus willingly gave His life for saints *and* for sinners because He loved with the perfect love of the One Who *is* Love.

At first glance, such love appears beyond our comprehension and even beyond our reach. After all, Jesus has a perfect nature and we do not. It is presumably easy for our Lord to love all mankind because He is, after all, the very essence of pure love. But what about you and me? Do we have the capacity to feel and understand God's love?

God Most Tolerant?

Our modern culture (and political correctness, specifically) suggests that God Most High is the "All Tolerant One." *God is love,*" some say. *"He loves and accepts us just as we are; He understands us. After all, He made us this way* [sexually promiscuous, homosexuals, substance abusers, liars, cheaters, etc.]. *He knows we cannot change.*" And while this politically correct view of God is convenient for those who want to go on sinning, no view of God Most High could be further from the truth.

Our finite minds cannot fully comprehend the intensity of God's holy, perfect, and selfless love; love that sacrifices its own—gives everything—for the sake of sinners. In our best effort to appreciate Christ's death on the cross, we cannot know or understand the depth of sorrow His Father felt, or the degree of pain that Christ suffered for the sake of our souls. It is because of God's vast and indescribable love that He cannot tolerate sin. S*in destroys the very ones that Christ died to save*, and regardless of what the current culture dictates, *sin is not relative* because God's Law will never change. God's Law is the result of His great love for us; it was designed to keep us from harm and to save us for eternity. The Bible is the Word of the Living God. The Almighty Himself instructs those who read it and blesses those who obey it. Though we cannot physically touch God, nor can we audibly hear His voice, we can know Him intimately and experience His divine love personally, through His Word, because His Word reveals His love for us:

Very rarely will anyone die for a righteous man, though for a good man someone might possibly dare to die. But God demonstrates his own love for us in this: While we were still sinners, Christ died for us. **Romans 5:7-8 (NIV)**

For scarcely for a righteous man will one die: yet peradventure for a good man some would even dare to die. But God commendeth his love toward us, in that, while we were yet sinners, Christ died for us. **(KJV)**

People of all different faiths believe that God is love—that He loves all people, ordains no harm to any, and welcomes all. And while it is true that God loves unconditionally, that fact cannot be separated from the fact that He hates sin as intensely as He loves sinners. God *does* welcome all people. Jesus said, *whosoever will,* may come—-but the "whosoever" was always conditional. "Whosoever loses his life for me…will save it…" and "whosoever will, let him take the water of life freely." (Mark 8:34-35, Luke 9:24, Revelation 22:17). In other words, those who come near to God must come ready to die to sin and be made alive in Christ; they must take the gift of salvation that comes only through faith in Jesus Christ alone. The "whosoever" that Jesus speaks of, are those who follow in His footsteps, obeying the *whole* Word of God. It is convenient to think that we can go on sinning because God's love will always forgive us, but such thinking is foolish and spiritually destructive. Sin separates us from God and when God is absent, love is absent.

Indeed, the need for love is likely the thing that most often draws sinners to God, but love is only one element of His whole, Holy and perfect nature. God's perfect love works in idyllic harmony with *all* of His attributes: perfect holiness, righteousness, sovereignty, grace, etc. God *is* love, but love is not security against sin. God's love cannot become a blanket we cling to; we cannot throw the presumption of God's love over our sin, thinking that it will cover our transgressions. God's love can never be separated from His holiness and righteous judgment.

The Lord detests the way of the wicked but he loves those who pursue righteousness.
Proverbs 15:9 (NIV)

The way of the wicked is an abomination unto the Lord: but he loveth him that followeth after righteousness. **(KJV)**

Agape love

Love is never verbally defined in Scripture, but Love Himself *demonstrates* it on the cross. First and foremost, God's love is sacrificial.

"For God so loved the world that he gave his one and only Son, that whoever believes in him shall not perish but have eternal life."
John 3:16 (NIV)

For God so loved the world, that he gave his only begotten Son, that whosoever believeth in him should not perish, but have everlasting life. **(KJV)**

But God demonstrates his own love for us in this: While we were still sinners, Christ died for us.
Romans 5:8 (NIV)

But God commendeth his love toward us, in that, while we were yet sinners, Christ died for us. **(KJV)**

Love is the essence of God's nature. The extravagant, unconditional, immeasurable love of God is what compels Him to do all that He does. Every event and circumstance that God allows in your life and mine happens because of His indescribable love for us. And while our limited intellect cannot calculate the height or depth of God's love, we can seek to understand it by studying Scripture.

The English language offers only one word for *love,* but the Greek offers several, each uniquely different. In the context of 1 John 4:8 (*God is love*), John used the Greek *agape* (pronounced ahgah-*pay*), which means self-sacrificing love—the kind of love that sacrifices everything for the sake of others:

I have told you this so that my joy may be in you and that your joy may be complete. My command is this: Love each other as I have loved you. Greater love has no one than this, that he lay down his life for his friends.
John 15:11-13 (NIV)

These things have I spoken unto you, that my joy might remain in you, and that your joy might be full. This is my commandment, That ye love one another, as I have loved you. Greater love hath no man than this, that a man lay down his life for his friends. **(KJV)**

Intellectually, we know that Jesus willingly gave His life because of His love for you and me, but who can justly and fully understand that kind of love? What finite intellect can wholly appreciate love that forgives its enemies and prays for its persecutors? None but God alone could have fashioned such a love, and none but the Holy Spirit can illumine us to understand it.

However, as it is written: "No eye has seen, no ear has heard, no mind has conceived what God has prepared for those who love him"— But God has revealed it to us by his Spirit. The Spirit searches all things, even the deep things of God.
1 Corinthians 2:9-10 (NIV)

But as it is written, Eye hath not seen, nor ear heard, neither have entered into the heart of man, the things which God hath prepared for them that love him.] But God hath revealed them unto us by his Spirit: for the Spirit searcheth all things, yea, the deep things of God.
(KJV)

For I am convinced that neither death nor life, neither angels nor demons, neither the present nor the future, nor any powers, neither height nor depth, nor anything else

For I am persuaded, that neither death, nor life, nor angels, nor principalities, nor powers, nor things present, nor things to come, Nor height, nor depth, nor any other

in all creation, will be able to separate us from the love of God that is in Christ Jesus our Lord.
Romans 8:38-39 (NIV)

creature, shall be able to separate us from the love of God, which is in Christ Jesus our Lord. **(KJV)**

Over all these…

Love is preeminent among the fruits of the Spirit. It is "the greatest" of all the spiritual gifts and the virtue Christians must "put on" over all the others; it is the virtue that binds all the others together in perfect unity (1 Corinthians 13:13, Colossians 3:14).

Can you imagine *peace* or *gentleness* in the absence of love?

When you think of a disobedient toddler, an obstinate teenager, or an obnoxious co-worker, can you imagine *patience* without God's love?

It is incredible to contemplate that Christ gave His life for His friends, but how much more to know that He laid down His life for His enemies? Should we ever be willing to die for those who hate us, we will know that we have attained the Divine love of Christ through the Holy Spirit of God.

In the absence of love, all action springs from the flesh. For example, knowledge is good, but Paul says that knowledge puffs up, while love *builds* up (1 Corinthians 8:1). Without love, knowledge creates pride and glorifies self. *With* love, knowledge brings glory to God as His word is used to encourage others. Paul also says that faith that releases God's power is *nothing* without love (1 Corinthians 13:2). Even if one is blessed with the gift of faith and never—not even *once*—doubts God, he is nothing in God's eyes if he does not have love.

Without the love of God, we "*love*" others only when certain conditions are met and our *patience* runs out as soon as we are inconvenienced. *Peace* only exists when we have what we want, and *joy* is only evident when circumstances are favorable. Without God's love in us, *gentleness, goodness,* and *kindness* are only possible toward those who "love" us back, and *faithfulness* and *self-control* are only exercised for our own benefit.

Conversely, the love of Christ says *I love you enough to give you everything I have. In spite of your sin and in spite of this circumstance, I love you enough to die for you.* In a Spirit-controlled life, it will be evident to all that God has (literally) filled us with His love by *pouring it into our hearts* (Romans 5:5).

Life Application: Chapter One

Day One:

Record your understanding of the statement that God is love:

What do the following verses say about God's love?

Jeremiah 31:3

Nehemiah 9:17

Psalm 89:33

Think of someone whom you have a difficult time loving…. (Take time with this; it's important.) What do you think is keeping you from loving him/her as Christ does?

Read Luke 6:27-30 and paraphrase what it says:

Being as specific as you can, how do you think God wants you to pray for the person you do not love? Use the space below to record your prayer. (You may share your answer in general terms with your group or you may keep it private, but it is important to record your thoughts.)

Day Two:

Read 1 John 4:7-12 and meditate on the verses. List some ways in which you can show God's love to others:

What two things can you say about those who love? (v.7)

What can you say about those who do not love? (v.8)

How does one come to "know God" more intimately by loving others?

Think specifically of someone whom you have a difficult time loving. What are you willing to do to show him/her God's love?

Day Three:

Study the verses in 1 John 4:13-18 and answer the following questions: How can we know that we "live in Christ?" (v. 13)

What does it mean to have been "given the Spirit of God" How should that change us?

What are we to do with the love of God? (v. 16)
In what ways do you rely on the love of God?

Day Four:

Read 1 John 4: 17-18. What do you think is going to happen on the "day of judgment?"

Why does an understanding of God's love give us "confidence" on the day of judgment?

What do you think John means when he says, "perfect love casts out fear?" (v. 18)

Read Romans 8:1-2. Do you think the believer should fear judgment day? Explain your answer.

Day Five:

What is the most significant thing you learned about the love of God this week?

Considering your answer (above), what changes do you plan to make in your behavior?

What will you do to insure that you follow through with your plan?

Chapter 2

Man's Love for God

"Teacher, which is the greatest commandment in the Law?" Jesus replied: "Love the Lord your God with all your heart and with all your soul and with all your mind. This is the first and greatest commandment."

Matthew 22:36-38 (NIV)

Worship is pure or base as the worshipper entertains high or low thoughts of God. For this reason the gravest question before the church is always God Himself, and the most portentous fact about any man is not what he at a given time may say or do, but what he in his deep heart conceives God to be like.

— A.W. Tozer

Christians are quick to profess love for God, yet few of us think deeply enough about what we mean when we make such a statement. Do we truly *love* God, or do we merely take pleasure in our relationship with Him? Are we devoted to Jesus Christ, or are we merely comfortable saying that we belong to His community of people? Do we appreciate God because He is holy and righteous, abounding in grace, mercy, and love, or do we value Him more because of what He can *do* for us? Do we love God enough to obey His Word completely, or do we obey Scripture only when the Word of God does not conflict with our personal desires and lifestyle choices? In other words, we can say we love God, but can we identify the *way* in which we love Him?

As we reflect on *how* we love God, we must also consider the reasons *why* we love Him. I believe that most of us first come to God out of personal need, and then we grow to love Him because of His compassion, mercy and faithfulness to us. To make the point, consider that we are born in the flesh, and we are born needy; we need others to teach, care for, and help us, and (according to mental health professionals) we need to feel loved by others. In much the same way, spiritual rebirth occurs when individuals seek God because they "need' something; they need to be forgiven, they need help or deliverance, or maybe they just feel the need to fill the void that exists in every human heart. In any case, they have a need, they think God can fill it, so they are drawn to Him. By way of contrast, when the Gospel was presented to me as a young woman, I remember telling the hopeful evangelist, *"That's fine for you, but I don't need anyone to take care of me; I can take care of myself."*

Presuming that the individual's need *does* bring him to God, we don't have to speculate as to whether God will welcome us on that basis. After all, Jesus came because of man's need for a Savior. And it was Jesus who said**, "Come to me, all you who are weary and burdened, and I will give you rest" (Matthew 11:28) ..."If anyone is thirsty, let him come to me and drink" (John 7:37) ..."All I have is yours" (John 17:10).** There is nothing that God the Father does not want to give us through His Son, Jesus Christ. God wants us to come to Him, regardless of what we need. In fact, as in my personal life, until one feels needy, he or she may likely never see their need for God. In fact, if God's blessings were not given because of our *need*, they would cease to be by His grace.

There is nothing wrong with needing God and appreciating all that He does for us, but there is much wrong if we fail to wholly value and reverence God Most High. The human need for God is innate; humans were created with a need to know Him (Romans 1:18-32). But deep appreciation and *reverence* for God comes only after serious contemplation of His character. For example, when I think of my life without Christ, I think of a "religious" but anxious, often obnoxious, insecure, bitter, and unforgiving young woman. Then I consider myself now, and I sincerely appreciate what God has done for me—how His Holy Spirit *in* me has created significant and positive changes in my attitudes and behavior, and in my quality of life. But when I go a step beyond the obvious and ponder what Jesus did for me on the cross, my appreciation for God ascends into the realm of a love so deep that it is indescribable.

Skeptic that I am, I began my Christian life as a student of apologetics. I have studied the historical accounts of the life, death, and resurrection of Jesus Christ. I believe the biblical version of those events to be historically accurate and scientifically viable because the Scriptures correlate with supplementary historical accounts. Further, I believe that if the testimony of Christ's life, death, and resurrection were presented in *any* court of law today, any educated, common sense jury would find the evidence sufficient to prove that the events happened exactly as Scripture details them. Because I believe intellectually in the reality of Christ's death and resurrection, it is very real to me. Insofar as I am able, I can imagine what it must have been like for Jesus to suffer and die for sinners. I can only imagine what it must have been like for Him to be spat upon, ridiculed and publicly humiliated. While few (if any) would *willingly* suffer as Jesus did, we can try to imagine the physical pain He felt being beaten, whipped, nailed to a cross, and left hanging by His arms to die. It is incomprehensible that anyone would love *me* enough to die like that—because of *my* sins. What did *I* do to deserve such sacrifice? What did *I* do to deserve such love? And why did God give *me* a heart to receive His gift of eternal life when so many others continue to reject the message of salvation through Christ alone?

The answer of course, is that I did *nothing* to earn God's love or my salvation. It is only by God's *grace* that I was saved, through faith. My salvation is not the result of anything I *did* or didn't do; it is a gift of God (Ephesians 2:8). That said, what began as my desire (or need) for a more meaningful and abundant life, has grown into a deep and abiding love for the One who meets my needs. Now, it is up to me to express my love in such a way that God is glorified by my actions. I must be more than a hearer of the Word. I must do more than just speak of my love for God; I must *demonstrate* it by obeying His Word and by living my life in such a way that He is glorified in all that I do.

Love the Lord your God with all your heart and with all your soul and with all your strength.
Deuteronomy 6:5 (NIV)

And thou shalt love the Lord thy God with all thine heart, and with all thy soul, and with all thy might.
(KJV)

"If you love me, you will obey what I command." **John 14:15 (NIV)**

If ye love me, keep my commandments. **(KJV)**

Praise and Worship

Pure love expresses itself through praise and worship to the Father, through the Son:

All the nations you have made will come and worship before you, O Lord; they will bring glory to your name. **Psalm 86:9 (NIV)**

All nations whom thou hast made shall come and worship before thee, O Lord; and shall glorify thy name. **(KJV)**

All you have made will praise you, O Lord; your saints will extol you.
Psalm 145:10 (NIV)

All thy works shall praise thee, O Lord; and thy saints shall bless thee. **(KJV)**

Therefore, I urge you, brothers, in view of God's mercy, to offer your bodies as living sacrifices, holy and pleasing to God—this is your spiritual act of worship.
Romans 12:1 (NIV)

I beseech you therefore, brethren, by the mercies of God, that ye present your bodies a living sacrifice, holy, acceptable unto God, which is your reasonable service.
(KJV)

Recently, a woman I had just met used the phrase, *"Praise the Lord!"* during a business transaction. Immediately after she said it, she looked me directly in the eye and said, "...*And I mean that!*" Such an exchange may seem inconsequential, but Charlene impressed me by taking the time to emphasize her faith. I thought, she must be a committed Christian.

It took a couple of days for us to work out the details of our agreement, and during that time Charlene gently revealed more about her relationship with the Lord: She told me "the Lord moved her" from Maine to California; she didn't know why at first, but God had really "blessed" her business. Her son was in the military and his unit was being deployed to the Middle East; she had "prayed protection over him," and so on.

Throughout the entire transaction, Charlene worked diligently, attending to every detail and following through with each promise she made. She was joyful (even when her commission was threatened), honest, and gracious.

She did exceedingly more than was required of her. And before our transaction was complete, Charlene told me about her church and invited me to a Sunday service.

Charlene's actions proved to me that her praise was genuine. She had sought to give God glory by working diligently, giving Him her best, and crediting Him for her success. Finally, she glorified God by reaching out to a stranger (me), not knowing what I believed, or whether I would reject her.

Phrases like "Praise the Lord!" and "To God be the glory!" are common in Christian circles. But sadly, such idioms are often trivialized because they are so frequently spoken. What is praise? And—in practical terms—what does it mean to glorify God? How does one make spiritual acts of worship a part of everyday life?

To extol means to praise, to glorify, or to bring glory to. Acts of praise are outwardly audible and visible. We may fold our hands in prayer, or we raise our hands in praise; we may sing, or verbally testify to God's grace and goodness. But we glorify God by extending our praise to include that which only He may see: trust (Romans 4:20), sacrifice (1 Peter 4:14), service (John 15:8), faithfulness 1 Peter 4:11), perseverance (Psalm 86:12), holiness (1 Peter 2:12), and obedience (1 Peter 1:14). In other words, man proves his love for God by what he does and how he reacts to the conditions of life. When man acts and reacts as Jesus would, he glorifies the Father.

But if anyone obeys his word, God's love is truly made complete in him. This is how we know we are in him. Whoever claims to live in him must walk as Jesus did.
1 John 2:5-6 (NIV)

But whoso keepeth his word, in him verily is the love of God perfected: hereby know we that we are in him. He that saith he abideth in him ought himself also so to walk, even as he walked. **(KJV)**

God's desire is that we love Him earnestly. The Father is resolute and specific regarding the kind of devotion He expects: *"Love me with your whole heart,"* He says. *"Love me more than you love your family, your possessions, your pleasures, or your life. Love me enough to obey me. Love me enough to trust me. Love me first, only, and supremely."*

Through praise, people make verbal professions of love for God, but it is man's *actions* that give spiritual life to his claim. We prove our love for God by what we *do*. Those who truly love God with all their "heart and soul and mind"[1] will walk as Jesus did. They will obey God, whatever the cost or inconvenience.

Love obeys...

Man's love for God, *if it is genuine*, will and must be marked by obedience:

And this is love: that we walk in obedience to his commands. As you have heard from the beginning, his command is that you walk in love.
2 John 1:6 (NIV)

And this is love, that we walk after his commandments. This is the commandment, That, as ye have heard from the beginning, ye should walk in it. **(KJV)**

This is love for God: to obey his commands. And his commands are not burdensome.
1 John 5:3 NIV

For this is the love of God, that we keep his commandments: and his commandments are not grievous.
(KJV)

The English word "keep" (KJV) implies watchful care; it means to *attend to carefully,* to take care of, or to *guard.* Genuine love for God goes even beyond obedience. Those who love God will be "*keepers*" (guardians) of His Word because they recognize and appreciate the value of the Holy Scriptures. Keepers of the Word must guard and teach the *whole and unadulterated Word of God.*

Sadly, liberalism has spawned many preachers who are diluting the Truth in order to accommodate the sins of our culture. Mainstream denominations are ordaining homosexual clergy, defending abortion, and ignoring every sort of sexual sin. There are many "Christian" pastors and teachers who speak on everything from Genesis to Revelation without ever mentioning the word "sin." Regardless of the personal cost, those who love God must protect the Holy Scriptures from being contaminated by the culture.

Do not add to what I command you and do not subtract from it, but keep the commands of the Lord your God that I give you.
Deuteronomy 4:2 (NIV)

Ye shall not add unto the word which I command you, neither shall ye diminish ought from it, that ye may keep the commandments of the Lord your God which I command you. **(KJV)**

All of Scripture is God-breathed (2 Timothy 3:16) and all of it is flawless (2 Samuel 22:31, Psalm 12:6). It is more than foolish for anyone to presume to "improve" on God's Word by modifying Scripture in an effort to trivialize or justify sin. When the Lord said, **"If you love me, you will keep my commands"** (John 14:15, John 15:10). His statement was unconditional. He meant *all of them.*

Love rejoices in the truth…

Those who love God must love righteousness and hate evil. One cannot genuinely love the Truth and remain indifferent to, or tolerant of sin—ever. The Truth is, *All* sin separates us from God. Scripture makes no reference to "small sins." Indeed, a tiny bite of forbidden fruit led to the Fall of man. Soon afterward, Eve's "small" sin was compounded in her children, and again in her children's children, as its consequences were passed from one generation to the next.

Regardless of the "size" of one's sin, certain things are true of all sin:

- All sin is the result of disobedience
- All sin separates the sinner from God
- All sin hurts someone
- All sin has consequences
- The more one sins, the less sensitive to sin he becomes
- We must confess our sin in order to be forgiven
- There is no sin that God will not forgive if the confessor is truly repentant

When you were dead in your sins and in the uncircumcision of your sinful nature, God made you alive with Christ. He forgave us all our sins, having canceled the written code, with its regulations, that was against us and that stood opposed to us; he took it away, nailing it to the cross. And having disarmed the powers and authorities, he made a public spectacle of them, triumphing over them by the cross.

Colossians 2:13-15 (NIV)

And you, being dead in your sins and the uncircumcision of your flesh, hath he quickened together with him, having forgiven you all trespasses; Blotting out the handwriting of ordinances that was against us, which was contrary to us, and took it out of the way, nailing it to his cross; and having spoiled principalities and powers, he made a shew of them openly, triumphing over them in it.

(KJV)

Oswald Chambers wrote that love for God "is the intensest [sic], the most vital, the most passionate love of which the human heart is capable." We are called to love God so much that the love we feel for others is *hatred,* by comparison (Luke 14:26). If we truly love God, we will love and obey His Word, and we will love His righteous Law.

Life Application: Chapter 2

Day One:

Read Deuteronomy 6:5. How does this verse instruct you to love God?

What does it mean to you to love "with all your heart, soul and strength?"

From whom does Jesus receive glory? (John 17:8-10).

How do Christ's followers bring glory to Him? (John 15:7-8).

How does one "remain in" Christ?

What does it mean to you to "bear much fruit?"

Day Two:

Read 1 Kings 3:3. How did Solomon actively demonstrate his love for God?

Read the following verses and record the ways in which we can glorify God:

Psalm 69:30

Psalm 86:9

1 Peter 2:12

John 14:13-14

Day Three:

Read Revelation 22:18-19 and answer the following questions:

What does God mean when He says He "will add the plagues" described in Scripture to anyone who alters His Word?

God says that if anyone "takes words away" from the Book of Revelation, he/she will "lose his share in the tree of life and in the holy city." What does that mean?

In view of what God says regarding those who alter Scripture, why do you think so many pastors and teachers continue to adjust the Word of God?

Day Four:

Do you think it is possible to genuinely love God and still break His Law? Give a *detailed* explanation of your answer.

How do you think God feels about those who profess to love Him, but do not obey His Word? (Revelation 3:15-16).

How will God judge those who profess to be followers of Christ, yet continue to live as the world lives? (Romans 2:6-11).

Day Five:

Read Deuteronomy 6:24-25. How does one acquire righteousness?

Read Isaiah 59:15-17. How is righteousness described here? Why do you think Scripture equates righteousness with a "breastplate"?

Read Matthew 5:16. Throughout Scripture we learn that those who love God will glorify him through obedience, service, and righteous living. What do you plan to do to ensure that others will see your love for God and glorify Him?

Chapter 3

Love One Another

"A new command I give you: Love one another. As I have loved you, so you must love one another. By this all men will know that you are my disciples, if you love one another." **John 13:34-35**

"Faith, like light, should always be simple and unbending; while love, like warmth, should beam forth on every side and bend to every necessity of our brethren." **— Martin Luther**

First Corinthians 13 defines the quality and result of "one another" love: **"love is patient, love is kind...it always protects, always trusts, always hopes, always preserves. Love never fails (1Corinthians 13:4-8a).**

In order for love to be genuine it must be actively demonstrated to others in specific ways. Indeed, the concept of Christian love would be a greater enticement to unbelievers if all who profess to love Jesus would love others as He did. The love of Christ seeks nothing in order to benefit itself. On the contrary, it abandons every selfish desire for the sake of others; it willingly sacrifices everything.

If you have any encouragement from being united with Christ, if any comfort from his love, if any fellowship with the Spirit, if any tenderness and compassion, then make my joy complete by being like-minded, having

If there be therefore any consolation in Christ, if any comfort of love, if any fellowship of the Spirit, if any bowels and mercies, Fulfil ye my joy, that ye be like-minded, having the same love, being of one accord, of one mind.

the same love, being one in spirit and purpose. Do nothing out of selfish ambition or vain conceit, but in humility consider others better than yourselves. Each of you should look not only to your own interests, but also to the interests of others.

Philippians 2:1-4 (NIV)

Let nothing be done through strife or vainglory; but in lowliness of mind let each esteem other better than themselves. Look not every man on his own things, but every man also on the things of others. (KJV)

Bible commentator Alexander Maclaren defines love as " the eternal form of the human relation to God. " In other words, when the Spirit of God is animate in one's heart, the gifts of the Spirit work together making Christian love visible. The harmonious interaction of *all* the spiritual gifts makes Christian love unique from any other as joy, peace, patience, kindness, goodness, gentleness, faithfulness, and self-control co-exist with the absolute, eternal certainty of God's love. Therefore, God's love never fails; it abides. Such love is an endless grace, because eternal love is its source. Of all the gifts we have on earth, only love will last (1 Chronicles 16:34, 41; Psalm 100:5; 106:1; 107:1 etc.).

The perfection of Love

In the 16th century, Francis Qaurles wrote that *knowledge of God is the perfection of love,* suggesting that the more we know of God, the more perfect our love becomes. This is true in that serious contemplation of Christ's sacrificial love for us will likely force us to ponder our love for others. Jesus died because of His love for us, but what are we willing to sacrifice for those we claim to love? What (if anything) are we willing to forfeit for our enemies? How inclusive is our love for others? Do we love people when they sin? When they speak ill of us? When they cheat? Do we love the poor? The sick? The obnoxious? The physically unattractive? Do we love those who criticize or falsely accuse us? Do we love those who are more successful than we are? How about those who disobey? How about those who intentionally harm us, or those who hate us enough to try to kill us?

I submit that it may be impossible for any human being to love everyone, under all conditions, with the perfect love of God because our flesh always gets in the way. We can love others if we *will* to do so, but that love cannot be "perfect" as God's love is perfect. For example, it is easy to love an infant at first sight because he is innocent and helpless. But when he cries and fusses, that affects, the *peace* in our home and we become irritated. Later, he learns to crawl and starts getting into things, and that tests our *patience.* Soon after that, Junior's running through the living room and knocking family heirlooms off the coffee table. Now, impatience escalates into anger and we don't always feel *kindness* toward him.

On his journey through childhood, Junior may test our *gentleness* and *self-control* by putting gum in his sister's hair or hitting a baseball through the kitchen window. Later, when he becomes a teenager, our *love* may be tried when he cuts school, questions authority, or backs the new car into a block wall. And when that innocent infant we once loved so "perfectly" grows into young adulthood, he will very likely make some choices we don't like. The question is: *how* will we love him then?

Our best efforts at Christian love may fail because our flesh struggles–at least to some degree–with feelings of resentment when others disappoint us. We may resent those whose sin hurts us–or someone we love. And when someone defies our spoken or implied will, pride often gets in the way of perfect love because our focus shifts from the *other,* toward *self,* since we view defiance as a display of disrespect. Conversely, when others comply by doing everything "right" according to our personal standard, we love them with little or no effort. Either way, our love is conditional.

By way of contrast, God's love is unrestricted. He loves everyone, all the time. And while we can please God and bless Him by obeying His Word, there is nothing we can do to make Him love us more or less than He already does. The highest objective of love is to love others as God loves us.

"I work in the public school system,"Shelly says, "...in the inner city–a testing ground for God's love if there ever was one! I teach tenth grade so I have mostly fifteen and sixteen year old students. I was twenty-three when I started my job, so of course I had all the answers, and I was going to change the world!

"I was an art major in college," she continued, "... and I had ... well ... let's just say I had a *unique style*. But I was way different from those kids. Most of them were pierced or tattooed, or both. And then there were guys like Fernando, who made his fashion statement by shaving his head and tattooing a gang sign on his skull.

"Most of the girls wore skimpy little tops, usually cut to expose their cleavage. Their jeans were low-cut and skin tight. I remember thinking that the goal was to ooze sex. Like the boys, the girls had a fondness for body piercing and tattoos.

"I wore my hair on the wild side back then, and I always dressed funky; nothing too crazy, but wild and colorful combinations; lots of bangle bracelets and big, dangly chandelier earrings. The girls often commented on my outfits and asked me where they could get something like it. I shopped at thrift stores, and they thought it was great that I could put such 'cool' outfits together for just a few dollars.

"I was pretty hip, and the kids liked me. I think they felt comfortable around me because I was young and unconventional. I was a fresh face and more like them than their other teachers. The other teachers were seasoned, well acquainted with the complexities of inner city kids, and likely weary of dealing with their problems. Most of them didn't enjoy teaching anymore; that was obvious. It was obvious to me and real obvious to the kids, whom I think resented most of them for their outward indifference.

"As a Christian, I thought teaching–changing lives–would be easy. After all, I had *God* on my side! I thought those kids would see Christ in me and realize that Jesus was cool because *I* was cool. I thought they'd all want to become Christians because *I'm* a Christian, and then everyone would live happily ever after! I thought that because I loved them with the love of Christ, they'd learn to love God, each other, and me in the same way. Boy, was I wrong!

"What I failed to consider was the fact that I didn't grow up in the inner city and I had nothing in common with those kids! I came from a comfortable home. My parents have always loved each other and they were committed to their marriage and family. No one in my family abused drugs or alcohol, and none of us abused each other. My parents disciplined sternly, but always with love. Mom would fix me a good breakfast before I went to school, and I always had a sandwich in my backpack for lunch. I just assumed everyone grew up like that. I didn't know how complicated life is for some kids. Nothing could have prepared me for what I saw repeatedly as a teacher: kids in filthy clothes, evidence of beatings, kids stumbling into class under the influence of drugs or alcohol...

"I never imagined that kids could be sexually victimized in their own homes, or that a some of them wouldn't do homework because their own children required so much of their time. I was naive and totally overwhelmed when reality set in and I saw how some kids live.

"In addition to art classes, I teach current affairs," Shelly continues. "I discuss cultural and social issues with my students. We talk about crime, abortion, sexual conduct, addictions, entertainment and the media and more. All of those are provocative topics for teens. Our discussions often become personal because all kids are affected by their culture. Once we were discussing an article about healthcare. Specifically, the question was whether taxpayers should be forced to pay for the prenatal care of unwed mothers. It was a normal, civil discussion until one of the boys rudely opined that if a girl was stupid enough to get pregnant (not the words he used) she should pay for her own health care. That infuriated two of the girls, both of whom had children, and one of them called him a filthy name. That provoked the guy's girlfriend, who returned the insult to the unwed mother ten-times-over, and within seconds, I had totally lost control. Before I could even react, some of the kids were out of their seats, threatening each other with words and fists. I had never heard such vile language, so vehemently delivered. Shoving started, and I ran down the hall for backup. It took five teachers and almost twenty minutes to restore order.

"I learned quickly that those kids have so much pent-up anger that the slightest thing can set them off. That experience, so early in my teaching career taught me the importance of praying frequently for wisdom and discernment. It made me very cautious about the types of discussions we have in class. I learned that *anything* can become a match that ignites one of their fuses, and explosions can happen any time.

"It didn't take long for me to become one of those 'seasoned ' teachers who was just going through the motions. My personal disgust for some of the kids began to affect the way I taught all of them. The 'helpless underprivileged children' that I had longed to help had quickly become obnoxious, immoral reprobates who seemed perfectly content with the status quo. My idealism was out the window. I didn't like those kids any more, and I didn't care if they learned or not.

"When my third year of teaching ended, I was praying about another job when the Holy Spirit led me through an unexpected spiritual diversion. I had been praying about *me*: *my* lousy job, *my* disappointment, and *my* miserable life, when God convicted me of my total lack of compassion for *others.* When truth revealed itself, I *recognized* it, and I immediately saw my own sin. It was a painful revelation because I've always thought of myself as one who has great love for others. I was stunned to realize that I *didn't* love those kids with the love of Christ, and it bothered me so much that I couldn't think about anything else for days afterward.

"It was summer break, so I had a lot of time to think. I wanted to understand how I could have had such a wrong view of the situation, so I began to seek God in earnest on the matter of His love and how I demonstrate it to others. The first thing I learned is that I was selfish and lazy when it came to the needs of my students. Those kids made me uncomfortable, and they made me work too hard at understanding them. I didn't listen carefully; I didn't make an effort to process what they were telling me because I had my own agenda. I wanted them to be like me–to believe what I believed and to live as I live because that made everything easy for me.

"As I continued to pray, I recalled things I'd said in class when I lost control of my temper, and I wondered whether my own harsh word had actually turned some of those kids *away* from the Lord? That thought was so devastating to me that I began to cry. What if it was true? How could I ever make amends?

"You see I had affection for those as kids long as there was hope that my expectations would be met. I thought they were just good kids in bad environments; all they needed was for me to love them and they'd change. That's what I expected. But then they started revealing their sins and that was all I could see. I stopped loving them and started judging them. I completely forgot about God's mercy until He showed me that it wasn't the kids who were disgusting; it was their *sin.* The kids were just imitating familiar behavior because they didn't have any responsible adults telling them it was wrong.

"The kids who were sexually promiscuous usually had promiscuous mothers. Those who used drugs usually lived with other drug users. Those who broke the law almost always had a family member who did the same, and the kids who hurt others were themselves hurting. I thought *if Jesus were teaching in my classroom, He'd introduce these kids to the concept of sin. He'd demonstrate His love by patiently teaching them the benefit of choosing to live righteously.*

"So that became my mission: to teach kids the advantage of living according to biblical principles. Love rejoices in the truth, regardless of what political correctness dictates. And I was willing to accept the consequences for teaching truth in a government school.

"By fall I had new students and a new attitude. On the first day, I set firm ground rules for all discussions in my current affairs class. I warned kids that vulgarities wouldn't be tolerated and I made it clear that points would be shaved form the grade of anyone who violated that rule. My rules weren't open for debate, and lost points couldn't be recovered.

"I wanted the kids to feel free to talk about anything, so I added that if I ever responded to them by saying, '*see me after class*' it meant that the question or discussion was inappropriate for mixed company. They were to drop the subject immediately. For the most part, that worked pretty well.

"I knew I had to build relationships with the kids before I earned the right to speak to them about their behavior, so I volunteered to supervise some after-school activities: I recruited students to paint sets for school plays and make decorations for school functions. I also started an after-school art club where kids could express themselves through art. The kids were with me because they *wanted* to be and not because the *had* to be.

Because the atmosphere was non-threatening, conversation came easily. They started talking, and I started listening. After a while, I started picking some of them up and taking them to church with me on Sundays. Since then, I am aware of seven kids who have accepted Christ. All because of God's love."

Shelly's testimony is about the unlovable, and at some point an obstinate child, an obnoxious relative, and insufferable co-worker, or an intolerable neighbor has tested each of us. Undeniably, it is a challenge to love the physically or morally offensive, the hateful, the objectionable, and the selfish. But regardless of how people look or how they act, God will give His people hearts to love the unlovable as Christ loves us. Jesus commanded us to love one another (John 15:12). His love was sacrificial. If we ask, the Lord will make us sensitive to the needs of others and He will fill our hearts with the compassion necessary to meet those needs. If we want to be like Jesus, we must *choose* to love, in spite of our emotions.

Life Application: Chapter 3

Day One:

Think of someone in your life who is difficult to love. In the space below, write a prayer to God about that person. Before you write, please ask God to show you how He feels about this person. What does God want for him or her? Who will meet the needs of this person on earth? Who will show him/her God's love? What makes him/her behave as he/she does? Is this person suffering? Why? What can you do to change your relationship with him /her? Please take time with this; it's important.

How does one identify a genuine believer? (John 13:35).

Read 1 John 4:11-12. Why is it imperative for us to demonstrate love to others?

Think of someone you know who does not have a personal relationship with Christ. (Someone different from the first question.) In the space below, record what you have done, or plan to do to demonstrate God's love to that person.

Day Two:

Why do you think we fail to love those who don't do what we want?

Read Romans 12:9-10. How does one know that love is sincere?

What does it mean to you to be "devoted to one another?"

What are some ways in which we can "honor others above ourselves?" (Romans 12:13-18).

Day Three:

As a Christian, what is your obligation to the believer who is suffering or who has strayed from the faith? (James 2:14-16 and 5:19-20).

Read James 5:20. Give this question serious thought before you respond: Why do you think it's so difficult for Christians to hold one another accountable for their sins?

What is the benefit of "speaking the truth in love?" (Ephesians 4:15).

Write about a situation in which "speaking the truth in love" would be difficult:

Think of a situation in which speaking the truth in love may not be necessary:

Day Four:
Where does truth lead us? (Titus 1:1).

What are the essentials for “speaking the truth in love”?

Proverb 29: 20

Ecclesiastes 10:12

2 Corinthians 4:2

2 Timothy 2:15

2 Timothy 2:25

Day Five:
What provides the believer proof that he or she has eternal life? (1 John 3:14).

Based on 1 John 3:14 what do you think about those who say they are Christians but do not love people of all races and religions?

How is God’s love made complete in us? (1 John 4:12).

What is the most life-changing thing you learned about love?

Chapter 4

Love Your Enemies

"You have heard that it was said, 'Love your neighbor and hate your enemy.' But I tell you: Love your enemies and pray for those who persecute you."

Matthew 5:43-44 NIV

"The believability of the gospel is tied to our loving in ways that sinners cannot love."

— John Mac Arthur

Each of us is born of an earthly father, and each of us has a spiritual father. According to Scripture, we are either children of God or children of the devil, but those are the only two options.

"Abraham is our father," they [the Pharisees] answered. "If you were Abraham's children," said Jesus, "then you would do the things Abraham did.

"You belong to your father, the devil, and you want to carry out your father's desire. He was a murderer from the beginning, not holding to the truth, for there is no truth in him. When he lies, he speaks his native language, for he is a liar and the father of lies."

John 8: 39, 44 (NIV)

They answered and said unto him, Abraham is our father. Jesus saith unto them, If ye were Abraham's children, ye would do the works of Abraham."

"Ye are of your father the devil, and the lusts of your father ye will do. He was a murderer from the beginning, and abode not in the truth, because there is no truth in him. When he speaketh a lie, he speaketh of his own: for he is a liar, and the father of it." **(KJV)**

As a result of Christ's words, many were convicted of sin and began to follow His example (John 8:30). To the new believers, Jesus said, **"If you hold to my teaching, you are really my disciples. Then you will know the truth, and the truth will set you free" (John 8:31-32).**

Jesus was speaking of freedom from sin, but the Pharisees missed the point entirely because they viewed themselves so highly. They kept the *letter* of the Law, but they ignored its *spirit.* You see, the Pharisees wanted to have it both ways; they wanted the benefit of association with God's family, but they didn't want the responsibility that came with that association. They wanted to *appear* godly, but they didn't want to act that way. When Jesus pointed out their sin, they became defensive. The Pharisees claimed to be children of God but they hated God's Son. Jesus was the enemy because He dared to tell them the truth; they were all sinners. In fact, they hated the Truth so much that they were ready to kill Jesus because of it (John 8:37, 40).

It may be difficult for us to imagine an enemy we hate enough to kill, but we all have enemies that hurt us. Some of our enemies will upset us with words, and some will harm us by their deeds. Some may injure us physically, and others will harm us emotionally. It's a fact of life that all who read this will be hurt by someone. The question is, *as children of the Living God, how will we respond?* Will we respond as the Pharisees did? Will we hate our perceived enemies enough to kill their bodies and/or their spirits? Or will we respond as Jesus did, and introduce them to the grace of God? (John 8:31-32).

Regardless of how we feel personally about individuals, God's will is for *all* to be saved, that they might experience His unconditional, everlasting love. And despite what others do to us, we are challenged to respond to their actions by showing them the love of Christ.

But I tell you, do not resist an evil person. If someone strikes you on the right cheek, turn to him the other also. And if someone wants to sue you and take your tunic, let him have your cloak as well. [41]

But I say unto you, that ye resist not evil: but whosoever shall smite thee on thy right cheek, turn to him the other also. [40] ***And if any man will sue thee at the law, and take away thy coat, let him have thy***

If someone forces you to go one mile, go with him two miles.
Matthew 5:39-41 (NIV)

cloak also. And whosoever shall compel thee to go a mile, go with him twain. **(KJV)**

In spite of one's actions toward us, Christian love always seeks the will of God for others because it acts in response to God's directive. We must love one another as God loves us (John 13:34). God loved us *when we were sinners* and He continues to love us when—even as believers—we fail to obey His commands:

But God demonstrates his own love for us in this: While we were still sinners, Christ died for us.
Romans 5:8 (NIV)

But God commendeth his love toward us, in that, while we were yet sinners, Christ died for us.
(KJV)

Therefore, there is now no condemnation for those who are in Christ Jesus because through Christ Jesus the law of the Spirit of life set me free from the law of sin and death.
Romans 8:1-2 (NIV)

There is therefore now no condemnation to them which are in Christ Jesus, who walk not after the flesh, but after the Spirit. For the law of the Spirit of life in Christ Jesus hath made me free from the law of sin and death. **(KJV)**

If we are going to love as God does, we must be generously merciful to those who sin against us.

And he passed in front of Moses, proclaiming, "The Lord, the Lord, the compassionate and gracious God, slow to anger, abounding in love and faithfulness, maintaining love to thousands, and forgiving wickedness, rebellion and sin….
Exodus 34:6-7 (NIV)

And the Lord passed by before him, and proclaimed, The Lord, The Lord God, merciful and gracious, longsuffering, and abundant in goodness and truth,] Keeping mercy for thousands, forgiving iniquity and transgression and sin,…
(KJV)

Do not repay evil with evil or insult with insult, but with blessing, because to this you were called so that you may inherit a blessing.
1 Peter 3:9 (NIV)

Not rendering evil for evil, or railing for railing: but contrariwise blessing; knowing that ye are thereunto called, that ye should inherit a blessing. **(KJV)**

When it comes to one's enemies, the flesh craves to return evil for evil and insult for insult, but Jesus never did that. Though He was oppressed and afflicted, the Lord never opened His mouth (Isaiah 58:7). When His enemies hurled insults at Him, He didn't retaliate, nor did He make threats (1 Peter 2:23). In fact, when the disciples offered to destroy His enemies, Jesus rebuked them (Luke 9:54-56). You see, as was the case with the Pharisees, the disciples weren't acting out of love for God or love for others. They were *re*acting out of pride and selfish ambition: they wanted to show the Lord's enemies that they had the power—through Christ—to destroy them. They failed to see that by physically killing the bodies, they were also killing the spirit, and thus destroying any opportunity for those people to come to saving faith.

While (hopefully) no one reading this would seek to physically kill an enemy, Christians can be as guilty as non-believers of killing the spirits of those who harm them. When Christians choose to return evil for evil or insult for insult, they choose to play the game of life using Satan's rule book. When we react as the world does, we obliterate all distinction between God's team and Satan's. We unwittingly link ourselves with the opposition, thus surrendering every opportunity to convince them that our side is better.

Ann never anticipated the extreme measures her unsaved neighbor would take in order to make her uncomfortable. From the first day Bonnie learned of Ann's faith, she sought to humiliate her because of it.

"The day we moved into our house," Ann says, "...my neighbor Patty brought me a cake and an invitation. Some of the neighborhood women got together once a month to play board games, and she invited me to join them. It sounded like fun and it was a perfect opportunity to meet my new neighbors, so I accepted her invitation.

"Patty introduced me, and throughout the evening, the women asked me the usual questions: Where had we come from? Did we have children? Did I work outside my home? What did I do in my spare time?

"Bonnie was seated across the table from me and when I mentioned that I taught Sunday school, she huffed obnoxiously and rolled her eyes toward the ceiling. Everyone noticed it. Then, as we got into the games, she cursed a few times and made an exaggerated point to apologize directly to me.

"Later, one of the women remarked that our house had always been her favorite on the block, and I said I considered the home a gift from God; the Lord had blessed our business, and with another baby on the way it was great to have more room. Well, by then Bonnie had had several glasses of wine, and *that* comment seemed to enrage her! She rolled her eyes again, slammed her palm on the tabletop and said: *'Oh pl-eeeeze; give me a break!'*

"Her rudeness shocked everyone, and no one knew how to respond to her. No one said anything, but their stunned expressions said a mouthful. She realized right away what she'd done and with all of us staring at her, she went on the defensive. She said, *'God didn't start your business! God doesn't get up everyday and go to the office and He doesn't put in sixty-hour weeks! If your business is successful it's because your husband made it that way!'*

"When no one responded she felt compelled to add that she hoped I wasn't *'one of those awful born-again Bible thumpers.'*

"Now everyone was *really* uncomfortable, and they were all looking at *me.* After a minute I admitted that I *am* a born-again Christian, I *do* study my Bible. Then I asked why that was so offensive to her? Apparently the question mystified her because she was quiet after that...until the next time.

"A few months later I was at a meeting at school when Bonnie walked in. Some of us were concerned about an explicit health-ed course, so my son's teacher invited us to discuss our concerns with her. As it turned out,

Bonnie had come to defend the use of the curricula.

"To say that the discussion was divisive is an understatement. The Holy Spirit enabled me to control myself, but I was so angry that I felt like hitting her. She mocked God's morality and she ridiculed my faith. Then she accused me of making an issue of the curricula in order to make a name for myself in the community, and she claimed I was forcing my 'puritanical views' on everyone else. And that was just the beginning....

"A few weeks later, I found out that Bonnie had been telling the neighbors that I was saying petty and hateful things about them. She even implied that I was secretly flirting with a couple of their husbands. Before I could confront her, everything came to a head at a neighborhood picnic when she acted so outrageously that I lost control. I'm so ashamed of what I said that I'm not going to tell you how bad it was, but it was a disgraceful tirade. And the sin was compounded because others heard me. When it was over, all I could think of was how I had destroyed my Christian witness.

"I thought my anger was justified, but the Holy Spirit wouldn't give me any peace because of the way in which I expressed it. I was convicted to the core and I knew I had to apologize. Bonnie's behavior wasn't the issue. My *reaction* to her behavior was the issue because I'm a Christian. I knew what I had to do; I just didn't want to do it. And for a while, I physically *couldn't* do it.

"The Holy Spirit wouldn't let me rest. I thought of my sin for days, mortified by what I'd done. Foremost in my mind was the realization that I had failed God—that He was grieved by my behavior. Secondly, I imagined what they must have all been saying about me: I was a hypocrite, a hothead, a fool for shooting off my mouth. I was miserable until I put my concerns for myself aside and truly repented of the sin.

"I did the easiest thing first: I asked God to forgive me. He knew my heart; He knew how truly sorry I was. Then I went to everyone who heard me and asked forgiveness. They all said I was making way too much of it. And when Patty's husband told me Bonnie had it coming, I said that didn't matter; *I'm* the one who knows Jesus, and *I'm* the one who must imitate

Him, regardless of what others do. Last, because this was the most difficult, I went to Bonnie and apologized. I don't remember everything I said but I told her that I was really sorry, and I meant it. When I asked her to forgive me, she said she'd have to think about it.

"Bonnie never asked forgiveness for the way she treated me and she never apologized for her gossip or for lying about me. In fact, things didn't change all that much between us. But a few years later, when Bonnie was diagnosed with breast cancer, *everything* changed.

"Bonnie had offended so many people for so long that few of them cared how sick she was. None of the neighbors went to see her in the hospital and only a few sent cards. So when she was sick from the chemo, *I* went over to sit with her. I wiped her face, took meals to her family, and encouraged her. And when she was too weak to protest, I read to her from the Psalms.

"I never told anyone about how I cared for Bonnie during that awful time, but *she* told everyone. They hardly believed it because they all knew how hateful she had been toward me, but they also knew of my desire to imitate Christ.

"Bonnie resisted God's gift of salvation for a long time, but she willingly received His love through me. The Lord continued to soften her heart and today, she's a different person. Partly because of what the Lord has allowed her to go through, but mostly because of His love."

Bonnie didn't just *hear* about Jesus, she *experienced* Him through Christian love. By the world's standard, Ann's story makes a classic case for vengeance and retribution. But if Ann had "done unto Bonnie as Bonnie did unto her," the story would likely have had a much different ending. As Christians, we are not responsible for the way in which others respond to Jesus Christ, but we *are* responsible for demonstrating His love. Ann showed God's love by dying to self. Pride told Ann to fight back because she had been unfairly attacked. She could have sought revenge, and she could have chosen to carry a grudge against her enemy, but she chose to follow Jesus, and do what He would do.

Life Application: Chapter 4

Day One:

Before you begin this section, read Psalm 51:1-7, and spend some time with God. Ask God to give you the courage to see the truth so that you can grow in the image of Christ. Now, answer the following questions: (Remember, this is your personal journal; you are not required to share your thoughts with anyone.)

Who is the first person that comes to your mind when you think of the word "enemy?" If no one comes to mind immediately, you are blessed. But in order to grasp the biblical principle, think back into your past…

Use three words to describe your enemy:

How do you think God feels about your enemy?

How is your anger toward your enemy justified?

Day Two:

Read Proverbs 25:21-22. In the space below, paraphrase what it says:

Now, answer the following questions as honestly as you can.

How did you respond to the actions/attacks of your enemy?

Do you think your reaction was pleasing to God? Explain your answer.

How might Jesus have responded differently?

Day Three:

Read James 3:14-15. Where do envy, bitterness and selfish ambition come from?

Read Job 31:29-30. What did Job think of those who spoke ill of their enemies?

How do you think you would you feel if something bad happened to your enemy?

Read Proverbs 24:17-18. What is the result of one's gloating over his enemy's adversity?

Day Four:

Turn to Psalm 35 and read verses 12-14. How did the Psalmist react to his enemies?

Instead of speaking hatefully or seeking vengeance on his own, how did the Psalmist pray? (vs 22-27).

List the advantages of allowing God to contend with your enemies:

Day Five:

How does God reward those who love their enemies? (Proverbs 16:7).

What fate awaits the enemies of God's children? (Psalm 60:12).

What does it mean to you to know that God will defend you?

Read Proverbs 10:12. Why is love always the best choice?

What is the most insightful thing the Holy Spirit revealed to you this week?

Chapter 5

Pray for Those Who Persecute You

Then he (Stephen) fell on his knees and cried out, "Lord, do not hold this sin against them." When he had said this, he fell asleep.
Acts 7:60 (NIV, Explanation added)

"When you love God you become identified with his interests in other people, and He will bring around you those He is interested in—the sinners, the mean, the ungrateful, and you will soon know by your attitude to them whether you love God."
— Oswald Chambers

Few punishments could equal the horror and physical pain of being stoned to death as Stephen was (Acts 7), yet at the moment of his death, the first Christian martyr was focused on only one thing: imitating Christ. An innocent man, Stephen had been criminally charged with blasphemy and taken to the Sanhedrin, the judicial council of that day. The Sanhedrin was made up of the chief priests and elders of the Jewish people, and they called false witnesses to testify against him. Instead of defending himself, Stephen smiled with "the face of an angel"(Acts 7:15), and gave the council a lesson in Jewish history. He reminded the "holy men" of God's faithfulness to the Jewish people and their failure to respond in kind. Then, Stephen called them "stiff necked" and asserted some charges of his own: they were resisting the Holy Spirit, persecuting the Prophets, and ignoring the sacred Laws they claimed to obey. Worst of all, they had betrayed and murdered the Righteous One!

We don't know how many of the Sanhedrin members were actually present during Stephen's discourse, but (including the High Priest) there were seventy-one members on the council (Numbers 11:16-17). When Stephen finished talking, they all became "furious and gnashed their teeth" at him (Acts 7:1-54). Then:

...Stephen, full of the Holy Spirit, looked up to heaven and saw the glory of God, and Jesus standing at the right hand of God. "Look," he said, "I see heaven open and the Son of Man standing at the right hand of God." At this they covered their ears and, yelling at the top of their voices, they all rushed at him, dragged him out of the city and began to stone him. Meanwhile, the witnesses laid their clothes at the feet of a young man named Saul. While they were stoning him, Stephen prayed, "Lord Jesus, receive my spirit." Then he fell on his knees and cried out, "Lord, do not hold this sin against them." When he had said this, he fell asleep.
Acts 7:55-60 (NIV)

...he, being full of the Holy Ghost, looked up steadfastly into heaven, and saw the glory of God, and Jesus standing on the right hand of God, and said, "Behold, I see the heavens opened, and the Son of man standing on the right hand of God." Then they cried out with a loud voice, and stopped their ears, and ran upon him with one accord, and cast him out of the city, and stoned him: and the witnesses laid down their clothes at a young man's feet, whose name was Saul. And they stoned Stephen, calling upon God, and saying, "Lord Jesus, receive my spirit." And he kneeled down, and cried with a loud voice, "Lord, lay not this sin to their charge." And when he had said this, he fell asleep. **(KJV)**

It's difficult to imagine that Stephen didn't fear death, especially at the hands of seventy teeth-gnashing, rock-throwing zealots, but he didn't. Stephen remained calm and reasonable because of his confidence in his eternal destiny. He had seen the glory of God. He had seen the "high and holy place," and he knew that Jesus waited there for him (Acts 7:55-56, Isaiah 57:15). I believe that at the moment of Stephen's death, God filled him with inexpressible compassion for his tormentors. At the same time, the Holy Spirit gave Stephen an instantaneous and fully comprehensive understanding of the eternal fate of those who *reject* Jesus Christ. It was genuine sorrow over the fate of his tormentors that led Stephen to pray.

His love was so like Christ's that he couldn't bear for even his murderers to suffer a pain so great as eternal separation from God. If only you and I could love like that!

Stephen's tormentors didn't know Jesus. They were children of the devil, behaving as the devil. The Sanhedrin's rock-throwing was simply an outward expression of their inward hatred of Christ. Their spiritual condition was so obvious that Stephen was moved to sorrow because of it. It was *sorrow over the fate of his persecutors* that led Stephen to pray for them. But what about *believers* who persecute us? What will compel us to pray for *them*?

Your Brother, Your Persecutor

Disagreements are inevitable within the church family. Everyone is persecuted at some point, and if God allows the harassment to come through a fellow believer, the way in which we resolve the conflict is crucial. The reality is, we persecute each other because every believer was born with a sin nature, and we are therefore prone to succumb to the flesh. If all Christians continually walked in the Spirit, we would do as Scripture suggests and resolve things peacefully (Romans 12:18) with each other. But *in the flesh*, pride sometimes exceeds reason, and so we choose to sin.

Mostly, Christians persecute one another with words. Verbal harassment of any kind always violates God's command to love one another. Still, we argue, gossip, accuse, and lie about each other, sometimes manipulating the truth in order to gain support for our point of view. In other words, instead of being controlled by the Holy Spirit, we allow the flesh to dictate our behavior toward one another. Instead of focusing on the person—the object of Christian love—we focus on the situation.

The highest value of Christian love is its effortless concern for others. It is a profound truth that because God controls everything that happens, His only concern is for people. If we will only focus on the welfare of the persons involved, instead of fretting over the possible outcome of the *circumstance* in which they're involved, God will (quite simply, usually) resolve the problem.

The second reason Christians persecute each other is that Satan *wants* them to. And as long as God allows the enemy to rule the earth (Ephesians 2:2 and 6:12). Satan will continue to bury land mines beneath the feet of God's people. When Christians battle one another, Christian witness is destroyed. Who will listen to the message of God's love if they don't *see* that love demonstrated in God's own family?

Do everything without complaining or arguing, so that you may become blameless and pure, children of God without fault in a crooked and depraved generation, in which you shine like stars in the universe as you hold out the word of life—in order that I may boast on the day of Christ that I did not run or labor for nothing.

Philippians 2:14-16 (NIV)

Do all things without murmurings and disputings: That ye may be blameless and harmless, the sons of God, without rebuke, in the midst of a crooked and perverse nation, among whom ye shine as lights in the world; Holding forth the word of life; that I may rejoice in the day of Christ, that I have not run in vain, neither laboured in vain. **(KJV)**

Infighting is one of Satan's most effective weapons of war. What better way to destroy our witness in this "crooked and depraved" world, than to persecute each other?

Resolving Conflicts

Scripture gives clear instruction in ways to resolve conflicts between believers:

1. *Resolve conflict quickly.* When we are estranged from one of God's children, we are also estranged from God. In fact, God will refuse even our worship if we are not reconciled to each other (Matthew 5:23-25).

2. *Concentrate on your common goal of faith in Christ*; that will put your disagreement into focus. For example, 2 Samuel 3 illustrates the way in which civil war destroys both sides. When Judah and Israel lost sight of God's purpose (to take the land and drive out the enemy), they began to fight against each other. Our common goal is to imitate Christ and share the Gospel. Conflict within the church always impedes our goal.

Be imitators of God, therefore, as dearly loved children and live a life of love, just as Christ loved us and gave himself up for us as a fragrant offering and sacrifice to God.
Ephesians 5:1-2 (NIV)

Be ye therefore followers of God, as dear children; and walk in love, as Christ also hath loved us, and hath given himself for us an offering and a sacrifice to God for a sweetsmelling savour. **(KJV)**

3. *Think of others first.* We quarrel among ourselves because of wounded pride and frustrated personal ambition (James 4:1). By focusing on loving the other, our eyes move off "self." It's not easy to forfeit what we want for the sake of others, but it is what Jesus would do.

4. *Approach the one who has persecuted you* (Matthew 18:15). In private, tell him specifically how he has offended you. Before you go, ask God to give you His right perspective on the situation so that you can see both sides clearly. Be kind and merciful. Demonstrate God's grace to others as He continually demonstrates it to you.

5. *If the persecution doesn't end, try again.* Only this time, take two godly people with you for counsel. If that doesn't work, go to your pastor or elders (Matthew 18:16).

6. *Regardless of the outcome, you must choose to forgive* (Matthew 18:21-22).

The biblical model for reconciliation is not negotiable. Selfish pride must always be set aside in the interest of demonstrating God's sacrificial love to others. It doesn't matter what our selfish flesh wants; it only matters what God wants.

Reasons for Persecution

Whether persecution comes from believers or non-believers, it is always spiritually beneficial. Sometimes, the Lord allows persecution in order to test our faith:

But he knows the way that I take; when he has tested me, I will come forth as gold. **Job 23:10 (NIV)**

But he knoweth the way that I take: when he hath tried me, I shall come forth as gold. **(KJV)**

For you, O God, tested us; you refined us like silver.
Psalm 66:10(NIV)

For thou, O God, hast proved us: thou hast tried us, as silver is tried.
(KJV)

Jesus said that those who suffer for His sake are blessed, and that our perseverance will be rewarded (Matthew 5:11-12, Luke 10: 29-30). Additionally, our suffering confirms the fact that Scripture is true. God never leaves us in times of trouble, and He is able to (and faithfully does) deliver us from difficult situations. Though we suffer, our love for those who persecute us must never grow cold because we have the hope of eternal life:

In your distress you called and I rescued you, I answered you out of a thundercloud; I tested you at the waters of Meribah. Selah
Psalm 81:7 (NIV)

Thou calledst in trouble, and I delivered thee; I answered thee in the secret place of thunder: I proved thee at the waters of Meribah. Selah. **(KJV)**

Because of the increase of wickedness, the love of most will grow cold, but he who stands firm to the end will be saved. And this gospel of the kingdom will be preached in the whole world as a testimony to all nations, and then the end will come. **Matthew 24:12-14 (NIV)**

And because iniquity shall abound, the love of many shall wax cold. But he that shall endure unto the end, the same shall be saved. And this gospel of the kingdom shall be preached in all the world for a witness unto all nations; and then shall the end come. **(KJV)**

Persecution also allows us opportunities to share the gospel that we may not otherwise have. A case in point would be Paul, when he was taken before Governor Felix. Instead of defending himself against the false charges, Paul proceeded to give the governor a lecture on self-control, righteousness, and the judgment to come. A more contemporary example would be the many opportunities I have personally had to publicly defend God's Law as it relates to cultural issues of our day. Because of the extreme liberal bias in the media, I am seldom invited to participate in a radio or television debate because the host *agrees* with me; I am invited so they can ridicule me for my Christian beliefs. And while I enjoy debating cultural issues, the intellectual ping-pong is always less exciting than sharing Christ. Mark 13:9 tells us to *"be on your guard."* And while I have never been *"handed over to the local councils and flogged in the synagogues,"* I have been verbally flogged countless times. During and after the public floggings, we must continue to love those who hold the whip. Persecution is the proving ground for Christians who want to demonstrate God's love. It's no challenge to love those who love us back and treat us well. It's quite another thing to love those who hurt us.

Weathering the Storm

Assuming that we accept persecution because of its benefit to our spiritual growth, it will be less painful if we study the biblical principles of enduring it. Regardless of the source or intensity of persecution, we must:

1. *Trust God and demonstrate love* (1 Peter 4:19). Whatever the situation, God is in control of it. He has allowed it to be and He can change it at any time.

2. *Be patient and demonstrate love* (1 Corinthians 4:11-13). In spite of severe persecution, the apostles not only endured hardship without complaint, they blessed when they were cursed. When they were slandered, they responded kindly.

3. *Be joyful and demonstrate love* (Matthew 5:12). Persecution is temporary, but love is eternal. Whatever the situation, rejoice and be glad, because great is your reward in heaven.

4. *Praise God and demonstrate love* (1 Peter 4:16). Because God works all things together for the good of those who love Him (Romans 8:28), our suffering is never in vain. We show others that our love for God is genuine when we praise Him and thank Him even as others seek to harm us.

5. *Ask for God's deliverance* (Psalm 119:86). Those who are persecuted for Christ's sake are never alone; God is near and God is able to deliver you. Ask Him.

6. *Pray for those who persecute you* (Matthew 5:34). This may seem to be the most difficult mandate, but it is a directive from the Living God. The Lord does not expect us to love our enemies in our own strength; the Spirit who makes the demand will empower us to do it.

God would never command us to do anything that His Holy Spirit cannot empower us to do. By continuing to love those who persecute us, we give glory to God by showing others that His love is not conditional. When the world tells us to hate those who hate us, and hurt those who hurt us, Christian love tells us that enduring love thinks of others first, and loves at all cost.

Life Application: Chapter 5

Day One:

List some reasons why people persecute each other:

Have you ever been persecuted unfairly? Explain.

Considering your answer above, do you think you were persecuted for Christ's sake, or for some other reason? Explain your answer.

Has it ever occurred to you to pray for one who is persecuting you?

How did you respond to the persecution? (Be honest in your answer; you do not have to share it unless you want to.)

Do you think the source or reason for your persecution changes the way in which God wants you to respond to it? (Yes or no?)

Day Two:

What are some common causes of disputes that may lead one believer to persecute another?

Proverbs 17:9

James 4:1-3

Philippians 2:3

What are some steps Christians can take in order to resolve a conflict between them?

Day Three:

What benefit is there in being persecuted for your faith?
(Mark 10:29-30).

Describe the apostles' behavior following persecution by the Sanhedrin. (Acts 5:41).

What did David do *consistently* when he was unjustly persecuted? (Psalm 119:61, 69, 78, 95 & 157).

Day Four:

What does God want you to do when you are forced to suffer for Christ's sake? (1 Peter 4:16).

Why do you think it's important to love those who persecute you?

Write your own definition of Christian love:

Day Five:

Regarding your responses to the questions on Day One: Considering all that you have read about persecution and how God wants us to respond to it, what would you do differently now?

Read *and meditate upon* Romans 12:18. Our disagreements with others need not be "serious" in order for them to grieve God. If we are gossiping about others, avoiding them, or doing anything else to harm them out of pride, our relationship with others is broken. Our relationship with God is broken as well. The Lord's desire is for us to live at peace with all people, all the time. Think of someone with whom you have a broken relationship right now…

You may not care if you are ever reconciled to this person, but *God cares very much.* If you truly want to imitate Jesus, use the space below to write a prayer for the one with whom you disagree. Before you begin, prayerfully ask for the Lord's perspective on the situation. Some possible things to consider:

- Ask God to give you a repentant heart and a *desire* to *pray for those who persecute you.*
- What part (if any) did you play in the conflict that led to the persecution? Ask God to show you your motivation.
- Ask for insight and compassion for the one with whom you disagree. Is he/she suffering? What does God want you to do to demonstrate His love *now*?
- If God convicts you of partial responsibility in the matter, ask Him for the strength to confess your sin and ask the other's forgiveness for adding to the conflict.

Your private prayer: (You will not be asked to share it, but you may be asked if you responded to the invitation to write it.)

Chapter 6

Love Forgives

"Blessed are they whose transgressions are forgiven, whose sins are covered. Blessed is the man whose sin the Lord will never count against him."

Romans 4:7-8 (NIV)

"Our Christian obligation is to forgive anybody who has invaded our rights, our territory, our comfort, our self-image, whether they acknowledge the invasion or not." **— Elizabeth Elliot**

All Christians are saved by grace, but we still sin. Therefore, it's impossible for us to *not* offend each other. And whether we are the offender or the offended, we must choose to obey the Word of God regarding the issue of forgiveness: we must ask for it, and we must give it.

Forgiveness comes naturally through *agape* love, because love that forfeits everything for others is already dead to self. Agape love resists selfish pride and puts *others* first; it extends God's mercy and kindness to those who offend, so that the Holy Spirit may lead them to repentance and reconciliation. *Agape love is the foundation of the Christian's obligation to forgive every offense.* And while love can't force an offender to choose repentance *or* reconciliation with the one who forgives, love is the light that illumines truth, and exposes sin.

Because each of us was born with a sin nature, our first concern is always for *self.* From the day we're born, we cry until our needs are met. Because we all desire to be content, our selfish natures will likely overlook the pain we cause others, while we dwell upon the pain that others cause us. After all, it's easier to visit someone else's sin, than it is to come face-to-face with our own.

When we're hurt, we are apt to dwell upon the offense long enough to feel good and sorry for ourselves before we remember that it's our Christian duty to forgive. Then, pride (not compassion) tells us that we're generous enough to pardon the offender. So puffed up by self-righteousness, we go to him and piously offer forgiveness. Later, when *we* offend another, that same pride keeps us from *asking* the forgiveness of the one we've hurt.

It takes two to disagree, so there are at least two perspectives in any conflict. Most differences would be quickly resolved if all concerned would simply focus on the welfare of the *other*. In order to resolve any conflict, we must pray for the *other,* and we must ask for the ability to see ourselves as we really are:

Search me, O God, and know my heart; test me and know my anxious thoughts. [24] See if there is any offensive way in me, and lead me in the way everlasting.

Psalm 139:23-24 (NIV)

The heart is deceitful above all things and beyond cure. Who can understand it? [10] "I the Lord search the heart and examine the mind, to reward a man according to his conduct, according to what his deeds deserve."

Jeremiah 17:9-10 (NIV)

Search me, O God, and know my heart: try me, and know my thoughts: [24] And see if there be any wicked way in me, and lead me in the way everlasting. **(NIV)**

The heart is deceitful above all things, and desperately wicked: who can know it? [10] I the Lord search the heart, I try the reins, even to give every man according to his ways, and according to the fruit of his doings. **(KJV)**

"*You* started it!"

Scripture never suggests that we should seek out an offender, express our feelings, and then tell the other, *but it's all right; I forgive you.* This truth is hard to accept if you are (as I am) candid in dealing with conflict. So I have to process it. I think it beneficial to deal quickly and forthrightly with problems because if we don't, small hurts may turn into painful injuries that never heal. But first, we must examine the *motive* behind the confrontation: Are we meeting the problem head-on in the interest of peace, or are we "telling it like it is" in order to call attention to what we perceive to be the other's sin? The former (I believe) is a blessing to God; the latter is sin.

If we are dealing with conflict solely in the interest of reconciliation, we must approach the other person with specific goals in mind. We must

- be affirming (2 Corinthians 7:4)
- be accurate and honest (2 Corinthians 7:14, 8:21)
- know *all* the facts (2 Corinthians 11:22-27)
- be gentle, speaking the truth in love ((2 Corinthians 7:15-16, Philippians 4:5, Ephesians 4:15)
- forget our own agenda and promote Christ's (2 Corinthians 12:19).

Foremost always, is the spiritual welfare of the *other.* If our effort will not possibly benefit him spiritually, we are wise to keep silent, and leave the matter to God alone.

Therefore each of you must put off falsehood and speak truthfully to his neighbor, for we are all members of one body.
Ephesians 4:25 (NIV)

Instead, speaking the truth in love, we will in all things grow up into him who is the Head, that is, Christ. **Ephesians 4:15 (NIV)**

Let your gentleness be evident to all. The Lord is near.
Philippians 4:5 (NIV)

Therefore each of you must put off falsehood and speak truthfully to his neighbor, for we are all members of one body. **(KJV)**

Instead, speaking the truth in love, we will in all things grow up into him who is the Head, that is, Christ. **(KJV)**

Let your moderation be known unto all men. The Lord is at hand.
(KJV)

Man's sin nature assures that, *in the flesh*, we do not see ourselves as we actually are. Instead, we see ourselves as we want to appear and so we deceive ourselves into thinking that sin is not our fault. But *in the Spirit*, we seek after *God's* perspective, asking Him to help us see people and situations through *His* eyes. Then the Holy Spirit imparts wisdom and quickly illumines us in ways to resolve conflict. Often the only thing needed for prompt reconciliation is the humility required to ask the forgiveness of the other involved. It's foolish and self-centered to drag out a conflict because our pride suggests that we deserve better treatment. *We "deserve" nothing.* It matters not who's to blame; all that matters is that the others involved know that God's love is greater than any dispute that comes between us. It is God's will that we live peacefully with one another (Romans 12:18), and when we make every effort to do so, He always blesses the outcome.

The Lord gave each of us free will, and however sincere our efforts to resolve conflict, some will choose to reject us. That fact doesn't release us from our responsibility to offer God's love by way of forgiveness; whether that means *giving* it or *asking for* it. Confession and repentance doesn't guarantee reconciliation with the offended party, but it does assure reconciliation with God.

If I ignore you, will you go away?

Cockroaches, cavities, and debts all have something in common with sin: they multiply when we ignore them. Any time we have a broken relationship with another of God's children, that sin separates us from God (Matthew 5:23-4). The adage "out of sight, out of mind" applies here. When we are separated by sin, we see less of God. The less we see of God, the less we *think* about imitating Christ. Instead, we lapse into imitating the world; we do as the world does; we hold onto negative feelings and thoughts. Anger and wounded pride keep us from forgiving and cause us to dwell on the offense. The more we muse over the offense, the more resentful we become. Over time, our resentment turns to bitterness that manifests itself in hateful speech, gossip, accusation and lies, as we attempt to "prove" that we are right. The progression can go on until we are living in a state of continual sin. At that point, pride has won out over love as our behavior demonstrates the truth: we care more about winning, than we do about the other person involved.

Forgiveness frees us from the bondage of sin because when sin is forgiven, the debt is fully paid (Matthew 18:23-27). There is no need to dwell on what is "owed" to us because we have forgiven the debt. In any case, forgiveness is not an option, it's a commandment:

"And when you stand praying, if you hold anything against anyone, forgive him, so that your Father in heaven may forgive you your sins." Mark 11:25 **(NIV)**

"And when you stand praying, if you hold anything against anyone, forgive him, so that your Father in heaven may forgive you your sins." **(KJV)**

The command to forgive seems illogical to those who do not understand the heart of God, but when Jesus said that all who want to follow Him must take up his cross (Matthew 16:24), He implied that the cross is heavy. It takes effort to pardon those who hurt us, but the Holy Spirit provides the strength needed to lift the weight.

What if I can't forget?

God forgives every sin, but He does not ignore our transgressions. Scripture is full of examples of the Lord's loving discipline and righteous judgment upon those who break His law:

I am with you and will save you,' declares the Lord. 'Though I completely destroy all the nations among which I scatter you, I will not completely destroy you. I will discipline you but only with justice; I will not let you go entirely unpunished.' Jeremiah 30:11 **(NIV)**

For I am with thee, saith the Lord, to save thee: though I make a full end of all nations whither I have scattered thee, yet will I not make a full end of thee: but I will correct thee in measure, and will not leave thee altogether unpunished. **(KJV)**

Forgiveness doesn't mean that I will simply forget sinful behavior, nor does it mean that the offender "gets away with it." God always holds sinners accountable (Deuteronomy 32:35; Romans 12:19), and since we know that God won't allow sinners to go unpunished, you and I are free to obey His command to "make every effort to do what leads to peace and to mutual edification" (Romans 14:19). My friend, Barb, says that when someone wrongs her, she often prays that God will lead them to repentance so that He can bless their lives with all His riches. In addition to this being a Christ-like choice that glorifies God, this makes perfect sense to me. It's not hard to pray that your enemy will repent, because that means that he is truly remorseful because of what he has done to you. Remorse means that he has the compassion to feel as you do; he understands that he has harmed you, and he is grieved because he did.

Christians have an obligation to acknowledge and deal with sin when it occurs (Luke 17:3), because love rejoices in the truth (1 Corinthians 13:6). Forgiveness means that I choose not to allow sinful behavior to negatively affect my relationship with the sinner. Once I stop focusing on the *sin,* I can focus on what's important to the Lord: the welfare of the *person* involved. It is awesome to think what would happen if every Christian, through wisdom and discernment, could fully understand God's love and mercy toward all humankind. What would our enemies think if we showed them the love, grace, and mercy that God has shown us? How would things change in our families? Our workplace? Our communities? Our world?

The cost of unforgiveness

Next March, Millie will be seventy-eight, but she won't be having a party. Millie has no friends, though she's lived in the same neighborhood and attended the same church for over fifty years. Mostly, she's estranged from her family. All of them have offended her, and she never forfeits a chance to tell anyone who will listen about their numerous failings.

Millie's marriage ended in divorce after thirty-nine years. She says he left her out of selfishness; he says he grew weary of listening to her berate him and others.

Millie "hates" her brother-in-law because he married her younger sister, whom (according to Millie) her parents always favored. Of course, she "can't stand" her sister because of "all the things she did" while they were growing up.

Only one of Millie's children lives nearby, but he seldom visits because Millie holds a grudge against his wife: Thirty-two years ago they eloped, so Millie wasn't invited to the wedding.

Millie doesn't like the pastor at her church because he was out of town when she had emergency gall bladder surgery; he didn't come to visit, and didn't even send a card! Still, she never misses church on Sunday. But she quit attending the Women's Bible study after just two weeks because a few of the ladies in her small group (whom she had just met) went out for lunch afterward and (sadly) didn't think to invite her. So she turned her back on the whole group and never returned.

Millie has spent her entire life nursing grudges against those who have offended her. She talks about petty grievances that occurred thirty-five, forty, *fifty* years ago, with the bitterness of one who experienced the event yesterday. She won't forgive because few have apologized for what she thinks is bad behavior.

Most of the people Millie "hates" (her word) aren't even aware of her bitterness. Others consider it a blessing. The fact that she's angry means they aren't expected to spend time with her.

Millie is blessed with intelligence, good health, and (really) a great sense of humor. She's a wonderful seamstress, and she paints beautiful watercolors. Millie is an avid reader. She knits, crochets, and bakes the best pies I've ever tasted. There are many things she could do with her life. She could go to the inner city and tutor a child, except that she is "disgusted" with minority groups because she's "forced to support them" with her tax dollars. She could join a book club, but she won't do that because last time she joined a book club (forty-three years ago), one of the women said something unkind behind her back. She could spend more time with her grandchildren but she "won't allow her kids to take advantage of her."

The point is: unforgiveness has a price. The price is bitterness, loneliness, and a loveless existence far removed from the abundant *life* Jesus wants us to have. Unforgiveness gives the devil a foothold:

If you forgive anyone, I also forgive him. And what I have forgiven—if there was anything to forgive—I have forgiven in the sight of Christ for your sake, [11] in order that Satan might not outwit us. For we are not unaware of his schemes.

2 Corinthians 2:10-11 (NIV)

To whom ye forgive any thing, I forgive also: for if I forgave any thing, to whom I forgave it, for your sakes forgave I it in the person of Christ; [11] Lest Satan should get an advantage of us: for we are not ignorant of his devices.

(KJV)

Though Millie is religious, she doesn't imitate Christ in her behavior. Those who truly desire to make Jesus their Lord must *never* give Satan the advantage by refusing to forgive others. If we refuse to demonstrate God's love by withholding His mercy and forgiveness, the one who is refused may become so bitter that he/she abandons the church completely. Then Satan wins.

Satan is a deceiver and the author of lies. He tricks unbelievers, and tempts God's children (1 Kings 22:21-22, 1 Thessalonians 3:5). He persuaded Eve to eat forbidden fruit, and he can persuade people to grow bitter toward God (Genesis 3:1, 2 Corinthians 11:3). Satan may easily persuade those who don't see God's love reflected in the behavior of those who know Jesus. When Christians are unforgiving, the unforgiven will likely see God that way because, after all, He is the one we are supposed to represent. The unbeliever will never accept the premise of God's unconditional love if he doesn't first see it demonstrated by Christians.

And where believers are concerned, failure to forgive can drive Christians to despair; *if God's family doesn't love me enough to pardon my sin, who will?* Satan is cunning beyond our imagination and when Christians sin, he will never miss an opportunity to multiply the sin. We must never give the enemy an opportunity to destroy our Christian witness; we must always choose the way of forgiveness, regardless of the cost to self.

Life Application: Chapter 6

Day One:
From where does forgiveness come? (Acts 13:38).

Read Ecclesiastes 7:20 and Ephesians 4:32. What do the Scriptures tell you regarding the issue of your forgiveness toward others?

After you have read and meditated upon James 2:10, record everything you think it says about the issue of forgiveness.

Day Two:
List everything the following verses teach you about forgiveness:
Exodus 23:4-5

Proverbs 19:11

Luke 6:37

Romans 12:20

Day Three:
What is the fate of those who fail to forgive others? (Mark 11:25).

Read Luke 17:3-6. When can we say, "*Enough is enough*" and rightly withhold forgiveness?

Why do you think the apostles asked the Lord to increase their faith?

What does Christ's response mean?

What should motivate believers to forgive those who hurt them?

Psalm 7:14-16

Luke 6:36-37

Mark 11:25

Day Four:
Ask the Holy Spirit to give you insight into this question and record everything that comes into your mind. Why do you think it's so difficult to forgive others?

Forgetting (only momentarily) what God says about forgiveness, is there a sin that you consider "unforgivable?" Explain your answer.

Consider the worst sinner you can think of…. How do you feel about the fact that God loves him/her with the same intensity that He loves you? Be honest and specific with your answer.

Day Five:

Read Colossians 3:13. After we have forgiven, what are we required to do?

What does it mean to bear with each other?

What does it mean to forgive as the Lord forgave you?

What is the most significant truth the Holy Spirit revealed to you this week?

Chapter 7

Friendship Love: Philia

A man of many companions may come to ruin, but there is a friend who sticks closer than a brother.

Proverbs 18:24

Friendship is "the happiest and most fully human of all loves; the crown of life and the school of virtue."

— C.S. Lewis

Unlike sexual love (*eros*), friendship love (*philia*) doesn't come to us accompanied by weak knees and a heartbeat that quickens when we see the object of our affection. And where *eros* occurs naturally out of biological instinct, *philia* grows (sometimes *un*naturally) out of common interest. We have work, leisure pursuits, neighborhood, faith, or something else in common before we choose to invest our time and emotions in building a friendship. Sadly though, our enthusiasm for making a new friend may wane once we understand the cost. Friendships require us to invest time and effort.

Once we've contemplated the price of friendship, we often decide that we'd sooner watch television, go shopping, or play golf because each will cost us less. We justify our selfishness by thinking *he lives too far away; it's inconvenient to meet with him.* Or, *she's too sensitive; I'm always afraid I'll hurt her feelings.* Or, *I didn't know how troubled she was; she's confiding in me, so now I feel responsible to give her counsel.* Suddenly we think, *maybe this friendship isn't such a good idea after all.* Then the next time the Holy Spirit brings that person to mind, we don't pick up the telephone. In fact, we may actually go out of our way to avoid engaging in conversation when we see our "friend" at church or in the grocery store. We can be certain that when the Holy Spirit prompts us to share God's compassionate love with another, Satan *will* tempt us to abandon a new friend or avoid an old one. Then we are wise to remember that *Jesus came and died for people.*

Do I need a friend?

All societies have one thing in common: the individuals who form the society *need* each other. For example, we can't always protect ourselves, so we need the military, police forces, and firemen. We can't heal ourselves, so we need doctors. We need teachers, farmers, postal workers, and mechanics. Human survival *requires* a cooperative community of *others*, but none of us "need" to be friends with those who help us, and usually we aren't.

Years ago I read a book on friendship in which the author suggested that most people are blessed if they have three real friends during their lifetime. He illustrated his point by telling the story of an elderly woman who appeared to have more friends than anyone he knew. This dear lady was an active member of his church, and belonged to an untold number of clubs, groups, and community organizations. Yet when this poor lady died suddenly at the age of eighty-two, not *one* of her "friends" knew her well enough to help locate her next of kin. It seems she had a myriad of acquaintances, but she was (presumably) too busy to build even *one* close friendship.

Despite the amount of time we spend in groups, few of us experience deep and meaningful friendships with individuals. Most of us aren't willing to sacrifice the time required to nurture such relationships, even though Jesus, our example, demonstrated the deepest, most profound kind of love: He died for us. God's love is unquenchable, unchangeable, and everlasting (Song of Songs 8:7, John 13:1, Romans 8:35). When it comes to humankind, the God of Heaven has no mere acquaintances or casual friends; He sacrificed all He had for humankind, because He loved us all so deeply.

Hopefully, Christians all show interest in the welfare of others because of a desire to imitate Christ. But most of us stop short of showing true compassion. We're thoughtful enough to inquire about Mary's recovery from surgery, but too selfish to go and visit her because that would take too much of our time. And we don't mind praying about a job for Mike, but we don't go so far as to pay his electric bill or buy him a bag of groceries because that would take our money. In other words, we "care" for others as long as doing so doesn't require much sacrifice on our part. By way of contrast, Jesus commands us not just to sacrifice, but to go the extra mile.

If someone strikes you on one cheek, turn to him the other also. If someone takes your cloak, do not stop him from taking your tunic.
Luke 6:29 (NIV)

And unto him that smiteth thee on the one cheek offer also the other; and him that taketh away thy cloke forbid not to take thy coat also.
(KJV)

The creation and cultivation of significant friendships should be a high priority in the life of every Christian because others will only understand Christ's compassion when they see it demonstrated by God's people. We should be so like Christ that others will seek us out as friends because of the visible way in which we care for, and about, others. Once we *show* God's love, others will listen to what we *say* about the God of Love. By investing time in people's lives, we earn the right to be heard. Building meaningful friendships creates opportunities for us to have the kinds of conversations that may change lives for Christ. Saint Francis of Assisi said, "Preach the Gospel always, and when necessary, use words." God's love must be seen before the Gospel will be heard and understood.

The face of friendship

If Michelangelo were to sculpt the perfect friend, he would carve the image of my friend, Jeanie. Jeanie is, first and foremost, a godly woman. I have seriously never met anyone who works harder at her relationship with the Lord than Jeanie does. She has been an example to me because of her diligent pursuit to be more like Christ, in spite of the fact that she suffers from more than one thorn in her flesh.

Jeanie is avid in her pursuit of God, and equally devoted to her marriage. I don't personally know of any two people who have put more effort into glorifying God in their marriage than Jeanie and her husband who are both devoted to individual ministries in their specialized fields, and they share a wonderful marriage ministry as well.

Jeanie is a compassionate person, and a great listener. Because of her devotion, study, and obedience to the Word of God, she is wise and discerning. In giving me counsel, Jeanie has never even slightly compromised the Word of God, and she always tells the truth in love.

Jeanie is an excellent wife and homemaker, and a wonderful steward of every resource God has given her. She never forgets birthdays, Christmas, or Valentines Day, and when she gives a gift, it is always beautifully wrapped and presented with flair, often accompanied by lunch. Jeanie and I pray together, and we laugh and cry together. Jeanie is kind, gentle, patient, and good; she brings out the best in me. Jeanie inspires me to seek God more seriously, and to share Him more generously. And as I watch Jeanie serve the Lord faithfully, she challenges me to use all the gifts He gave me to minister to the needs of others.

The child in me wants to think that I'm Jeanie's best friend and that she treats me more specially than she treats her other friends, but I know that isn't so. Jeanie has several other friends whom I know receive the same degree of attention and love that she gives me, and that's what makes her so exceptional. Each of us thinks that Jeanie "loves us best!"

Excepting the examples set by Jesus, Jeanie has taught me more than anyone about the meaning of friendship. And by reading God's word and observing my friend Jeanie, I am learning to be a better friend to others.

I am blessed to have many wise and godly friends, all of whom continue to teach me about the grace, compassion, and mercy of God. Each has taught me something different: Bev taught me the importance of being approachable. Though she is a pastor's wife, a mother, and grandmother with scarcely a moment to herself, she is never too busy to talk to anyone who needs a compassionate ear.

Lyndel taught me about hospitality: she's a wonderful cook, generous and lavish when she entertains. Lyndel's effort is obvious when guests enter her home; she goes out of her way to make each individual feel special. Above all, Lyndel seeks the will of God in her life.

Deborah taught me about the importance of persevering in prayer. She is a prayer warrior, and an example of what it means to trust in the Lord with all your heart. She is one of the kindest, most thoughtful people I know.

My friend Nancy is a bold contender for the faith, and a strong advocate for Truth. She loves me enough to hold me accountable, and I have grown spiritually because she speaks the truth in love. She is a great encourager, and she is always supportive of my efforts.

Patti has a servant's heart. She spends hours on church and community events, giving wedding and baby showers, and opening her beautiful home in an effort to give joy to others and help them succeed. She is extremely generous, always willing to help, and she never seeks recognition.

The Lord brought Pam and me together because of a concern we share, and as a result of praying for each other we have become extremely close. She lives far away and I don't see her much, but I think of her often and fondly. I don't think I have ever spoken to Pam when she didn't begin the conversation by saying, *"I've been praying for you."*

Space won't permit me to list the names and qualities of all my friends. I mentioned the names above because each exemplifies a specific component in the biblical model for friendship. Whether we are the friend or the befriended, Scripture provides directives for us to follow.

A friend who sticks closer than a brother

It is God's will for us to show His love and compassion to others, so no effort to befriend another is spent in vain. A friendship is like a rosebush; when it's not carefully tended, its blossoms become wilted and spent. Friendships must be cultivated if they are going to grow into the kind of relationships that glorify God. We aren't born a friend; we must learn to be one by studying God's Word. Following are just some of the Scriptures that define the quality of genuine friendship:

- True friends share one another's suffering: Psalm 35:13-14.
- True friends are loyal: Psalm 55:12-14.
- True friends are sincere: Proverbs 18:24
- True friends will never betray a confidence: Proverbs 11:13.
- True friends are always gracious: Proverbs 17:9
- True friends love unconditionally: Proverbs 17:17
- True friends love the Truth: Proverbs 27:9
- True friends are not overbearing: Proverbs 25:17
- True friends will always have your best interest at heart, so they will tell you the truth in love, even if that means you may become angry: Proverbs 22:11 and 27:6
- True friends will bring out the best in you: Proverbs 27:17
- True friends will help, encourage, and protect you. Ecclesiastes 4:9-12
- True friends are faithful: Proverbs 25:19

Investing time wisely

The most common excuse to justify one's lack of friends is "time:" *I don't have the time to develop meaningful relationships.* One way to create the time needed for friendships is to evaluate the relationships we already have. We may spend so much time in wrong relationships, that we miss God's invitation to invest time in the right ones. For example, my life was quite different before I became a Christian. I did things that didn't please God, and kept company with people who didn't think about sin. When I became a believer I didn't want others tempting me to continue the behaviors of my old life, so I asked the Lord to keep me from anyone who might hinder my spiritual growth. God responded quickly to this prayer (because He knows how weak I am) by systematically removing my unbelieving, morally confused friends one by one, until only a few remained. Those few have heard the Gospel, and while none of the three has accepted Christ, they have continued (as good friends do) to confide in me for almost twenty-five years. In that time, each has heard me apply biblical principles to life's problems and I honestly believe those morsels of God's Word have had a positive effect on some of their decisions. A good example is my friend who told me she was going to divorce her husband of fourteen years. After we talked, she said she had never thought about divorce as a sin. She decided to stay in the marriage, and try to work things out.

We all invest time in those who don't know Christ, hoping that we might influence them to accept God's free gift of salvation. We must persevere in such relationships (as long as we have peace in doing so) because we may be the only reflection of Christ that person sees. But we are wise to remember that God gave each of us free will, and not everyone will accept Jesus. Relationships with unbelievers can be time-consuming and emotionally exhausting. They can even be spiritually detrimental if the relationship (or the circumstance that brings us into it) tempts us to sin.

Years ago, I counseled a teenager who had just been released from the bonds of Satanism. One day, after we had met a few times, she told me that she was on her way to the local video arcade. The news alarmed me because I know that cults use those arcades as recruitment centers. (In fact, she had been recruited there herself.) When I asked her why she was going, she said she meant to share the Gospel. And while that's a virtuous desire, I suggested that it was a bad idea because she was a new believer; perhaps not mature enough in her faith to withstand the spiritual warfare that would certainly take place if she returned to that battleground. She thought I was foolish, and she continued to return to the arcade until she was finally sucked back into the occult.

The Great Commission is to "make disciples of all nations" (Matthew 28:19), and that certainly requires us to spend time with unbelievers. Our Christian responsibility is always to demonstrate God's love, but if one overtly rejects Christ, it's not wise to jeopardize our witness, compromise our beliefs, or misuse the time God gives us by continuing a close association. Satan loves to distract us in that way. When we're repeating truth to one who refuses to believe, we aren't sharing truth with another who may accept it. When it's obvious that we're not the one God wants to use to influence another for Christ, we are obliged to do three things: 1) love them,

2) pray for them, and 3) make sure they know that we're available if they decide to change their lives.

We must rely on discernment to tell us when it's time to move away from a relationship. We must ask ourselves: *Have I presented the Gospel clearly, and have I done everything possible to make it appealing? How persuasive was I in sharing my faith? Do I live my faith? Did I demonstrate God's love, or just tell of it? Do the circumstances in this person's life merit that I give it another try? Could someone else be more effective than I was, in reaching him/her?*

None of us has the time, strength or means to meet the emotional and physical needs of everyone around us. We cannot give quality time to everyone, all the time. And frankly, there are many who don't care about a transformed life; they simply want someone to listen to their problems, which often result from sinful behavior they don't want to change.

While we can choose our friends, we can't choose the relatives, co-workers and neighbors with whom we must spend time. So regardless of what they believe, we are called to love them unconditionally, to always be kind and gracious in speech and deeds, and to be an example of Christ in all circumstances.

***Be wise in the way you act toward outsiders; make the most of every opportunity.* Colossians 4:5 (NIV)**

***Walk in wisdom toward them that are without, redeeming the time.* (KJV)**

Friends influence us, and not always in positive ways. If we keep company with those who don't see the importance and necessity of life in Christ, we may find ourselves lapsing back into life without Him. There are only two kinds of people: those who stand for God, and those who fall without Him.... those who love God, and those who love the world.

Life Application: Chapter 7

Day One:

How many close friends do you have?_____

What are some things you can do in order to stimulate friendship with others?

According to Scripture, what kinds of people make the best friends? (Proverbs 13:20).

What makes a person "wise?" (Psalm 111:10).

Do you think unbelievers can possess wisdom? Explain your answer.

List three people *outside of your family* whom you consider to be your closest friends:

Which of your friends knows the most about you?

What particular qualities does he/she possess that make it easy for you to share personal information with him/her?

Day Two:

Read Psalm 55:12-14. Why is the Psalmist so distressed?

Do you think it's more painful when a fellow Christian offends you? Explain your answer.

When someone offends you, what steps do you think the Lord wants you to take in order to resolve the matter?

Why is it wrong to repeat the transgressions of others? (Isaiah 59:3, Romans 3:10).

Read Proverbs 17:17 and explain what it means to you.

What does Proverbs 22:11 teach you about friendship?

Day Three:

What one quality is most important to you in a friend? Explain your answer.

Record the name of someone with whom you would like to nurture a friendship:

What do you plan to do in order to stimulate growth in that relationship?

Day Four:

Read the following verses and paraphrase what each says about friendship:

Proverbs 17:9

Proverbs 18:24

Proverbs 22:11

Proverbs 22:24

Why do you think some people have more friends than others?

Day Five:

What new insight has the Holy Spirit revealed to you this week about the issue of friendship?

Think of someone whom you think is lonely. *You will not be asked to share the name.* What do you think Jesus would like you to do in order to show His compassion to him/her?

What are some things you plan to do in order to be a better friend to others?

Chapter 8

Sexual Love: Eros

Place me like a seal over your heart, like a seal on your arm; for love is as strong as death, its jealousy unyielding as the grave. It burns like blazing fire, like a mighty flame. **Song of Songs 8:6 (NIV)**

"It is in the grandeur of Eros that the seeds of danger are concealed."
— C.S. Lewis

Eros is a Greek word that defines the *passion* of love; it's the kind of love that lovers feel for one another. Eros goes beyond feelings of affection; it's an intense longing to be physically and wholly "one" with another. Eros is the most profound and inclusive of all the loves, symbolizing the joining of one's body, soul, and spirit with another.

Eros is the intense longing for another that can cause one to become physically sick, and weak in the knees. It's a passion so powerful that it will do anything for the object of its affection, and that's precisely what makes it so dangerous. Eros may entice a lover to evil, as well as to good. One need only look to Romeo and Juliet, or David and Bathsheba to understand the ill effects of Eros.

In the physical realm, Eros is a passion so strong that it can persuade lovers to sin. Suicides, murder, deceit… treacheries of all sorts have upshot from the root of passion that began with Eros love. Multitudes of personal testimonies and "based on a true story" television movies prove that Eros can blind lovers to the truth, so much so that passion conquers common sense.

Less seriously, Eros feelings can be so strong that they persuade lovers to stay together, even though they know they won't be happy. They know that apart from physical attraction they have absolutely nothing in common. Many failed marriages began with Eros, as young lovers decided they'd rather be miserable together than happy with someone else.

Eros can also be spiritually perilous because, when it's most intense, it tends to fight against all else (including God) for one's affection. Eros may entice one to worship its object, putting the Eros relationship before one's relationship with a jealous and holy God. Then, "love" becomes idolatry that may lead some to sacrifice purity for pleasure as they offer their bodies (without benefit of marriage) for the sake of pleasing the beloved. So, you see, Eros is always sincere, but it is not always good. In order for Eros to be good, it must be love by God's definition.

The word *Eros* is used throughout Scripture to describe God's passionate love for His people. And while the Song of Songs is an allegory of God's love for us, it is also an affirmation of the marriage covenant as Scripture tells in very sensual terms of Solomon's *Eros* love for his bride. In God's plan, the physical union of a man and woman is meant to take place only within the confines of marriage. The act of sexual intercourse was intended to be a sacred means of celebrating Eros love. It was preordained to be pleasurable and is, of course, the only means by which children can be conceived and families begun. Unlike friendship love, Eros takes little or no effort. When the "chemistry" is there, we feel this passion naturally.

In God's plan, *Eros* makes a man or woman desire *one specific person* for many different reasons, and sexual yearning is only part of that. God pleasing Eros desires the other not because of the pleasure the other gives, but because the beloved is esteemed and desired apart from his or her ability to fulfill a need.

God created us with a desire for sexual intimacy and without it, the human race could not continue. But God's perfect plan for a pure union between one man and one woman within the confines of marriage has been so polluted that few can even imagine "being with" only one other person on earth. The problem with Eros love, is that we don't think correctly about it.

"Love" in the twenty-first century

As a culture, we largely ignore sexual sin. In fact, it's become such an accepted phase of the dating ritual that statistically, there's not much difference in the amount of sexual sin in Christian and secular communities. Many Christian men and women are having sex out of wedlock, and many are having extramarital affairs. There are Christian homosexuals who understand that *acting* on the desire for same-sex intimacy is a sin, but because Eros is so strong, they sin anyway, refusing to believe they have the power to resist. Eros can and does exist between members of the same sex, but Scripture is clear that God does not sanction (in fact, He "detests") sexual activity between same-gender people (Leviticus 18:22, 20:13, Romans 1:26-27, 1 Corinthians 6:9).

Whatever the type of sexual sin that originates with Eros, Christians continue in that sin for only one reason: because they want to. Anyone who has made Jesus Christ the Lord of his/her life has the power through the Holy Spirit of the Living God to resist *any* sin. However powerful the Eros emotion is, the power of God to enable holy living is greater. It need only be desired.

Those who choose to sin with their bodies *in spite of the Holy Spirit's presence*, will always find justification for doing so. Maybe they've been unduly influenced by the evolutionist's lies. Although Scripture says otherwise, they've been persuaded that they really *aren't* created in the image of God. Instead, they're only the highest form of the animal life He created. Therefore, they shouldn't be expected to control their biological—or "animal"—instinct to copulate.

Still other religious people have fallen victim to liberal theology, which suggests that since the Bible was written thousands of years ago, it's hardly relevant for life in the twenty-first century. Scripture is nice, and sometimes even helpful as long as it doesn't contradict one's lifestyle. But surely, God didn't mean for individuals to take it *literally!*

There are also devout Christians who read and study Scripture, go to church every Sunday, and honestly believe that God doesn't care about their sexual sin because "God knows the heart." They reason that because God "knows they truly love each other," their sin is justified. Such thinking is dangerously foolish and completely contradictory to what God actually says:

"Food for the stomach and the stomach for food"—but God will destroy them both. The body is not meant for sexual immorality, but for the Lord, and the Lord for the body. **1 Corinthians 6:13 (NIV)**

Meats for the belly, and the belly for meats: but God shall destroy both it and them. Now the body is not for fornication, but for the Lord; and the Lord for the body. **(KJV)**

God cares deeply about sexual sin because it destroys the lives of His people:

Flee from sexual immorality. All other sins a man commits are outside his body, but he who sins sexually sins against his own body. **1 Corinthians 6:18 (NIV)**

Flee fornication. Every sin that a man doeth is without the body; but he that committeth fornication sinneth against his own body. **(KJV)**

No container is big enough to hold the broken hearts of all the lovers who compromised God's law because of a false perception of Eros love. God's holiness will not allow Him to bless relationships that contradict His will for purity. However "wonderful" such unions seem at the time, all will eventually have consequences because sin is never without effect. Further, Eros—if it is Eros by God's definition—would never lead its beloved to sin:

"Everything is permissible"—but not everything is beneficial. "Everything is permissible"—but not everything is constructive. [24] Nobody should seek his own good, but the good of others. **1 Corinthians 10:23-24 (NIV)**

All things are lawful for me, but all things are not expedient: all things are lawful for me, but all things edify not. [24] Let no man seek his own, but every man another's wealth. **(KJV)**

The value of love

Eros (though the world has spoiled its intent) speaks more to the *value* of the sexual act than it does to the carnal aspect. Without Eros, the desire is for the act itself, because of the physical or emotional gratification it brings. *With* Eros, the desire is for the beloved; one yearns for physical and spiritual intimacy because he or she has assessed a certain *value* to the other. To be sure, Eros can exist without sexual intimacy, and sexual intimacy can (and certainly does) occur without Eros. So the question becomes: is sex without Eros wrong?

Years ago, marriages were often arranged. Undoubtedly, some of those brides and grooms were not sexually attracted to each other. And since (in many cases) they scarcely knew each other, there was little opportunity for Eros to grow between them before marriage. But once they married, they had sexual relations without Eros because the marriage "duty" was necessary in order for them to start a family. And even in the absence of Eros, they had God's blessing because they had, in obedience to His Word, made a legal commitment to one another.

Additionally, there are many long-married couples that don't feel the same desire for intimacy they once did. So when one of them feels "frisky" and the other doesn't, the one less eager will acquiesce even though the Eros passion isn't there.

On the other hand, we shouldn't study Eros without reminding the young that years ago, people married simply *because* of it. The moral climate was such that marriage outside of wedlock was frowned upon. "Nice" girls wouldn't give their bodies away, so some couples married only because of the "chemistry," learning too late that friendship and spiritual compatibility are far more important than physical attraction. In any of the aforementioned cases, the sexual act was part of the *commitment* the couple made to one another in the sight of God. So the answer is, *"No. Sexual relations without Eros are not sinful as long as there is a marriage commitment."*

Today, when we hear the words "commit" or "commitment" as pertaining to relationships, they're usually preceded by words like "failure to" and "lack of." The failure (mostly by men) to commit to marriage is due, for the most part, to one recurring factor: they don't have to. Sexual gratification is no longer a reason for men to marry because they can pretty much have sex at will with numerous partners if they just know where to look. In today's culture, "making love" has become a euphemism for carnal sex. As the term is thrown around, it seldom means there is Eros (or any other kind of) love involved. More likely, two acquaintances mutually decide to engage in sensual pleasure for their own selfish reasons. A man will "make love" to a woman simply because she has what he needs in order to complete the act. He doesn't have to love her, and when the act is over, he makes his true feelings known. (Few will keep the wrapping once they've had the present.)

While some women share the male's biological urge to "make love," most have multiple partners for other reasons, "multiple" meaning more than the *one* God intended. Research shows that many promiscuous women are compensating for what they perceive to be their father's lack of interest in them. What they *really* desire, is the closeness of a man. Any man. (Fathers must pay close attention to this reality. Satan wants us to deny that this problem exists, but mental health professionals assure us it does. And while little boys are just as important as little girls, the *needs* of young girls are quite different.)

Another factor adding to increased sexual promiscuity is Women's Studies curricula that unashamedly encourage women to use their bodies as a means to gain power over men. Few deny that some women use sex to barter for material gain: *This guy is good looking and successful; if I don't give him what he wants, he may drop me and find someone else.*

Other women report that the sexual act makes them feel desirable, or attractive, or needed. Whatever the reason, Christian men and women are quick to ignore God's desire and command for pure relationships in order to get what they want. But we must understand that in that regard, the act of sexual intercourse has nothing to do with the Eros love as God designed it.

Don't kill the messenger

It's quite unpopular to suggest that God's Word, with all its demands for purity and holy living, is still relevant in the twenty-first century. In fact, we are living in an Age of Moral Relativism. Here, individuals are encouraged to write their own code of behavior.

Even among those who identify themselves as "Evangelical Christians," less than 50% actually believe in absolute truth. Many Evangelicals love God's Word in that it promises eternal life and multitudes of blessings for those who believe. But they don't love it well enough to obey the parts of Scripture that command them to be holy, as God is holy (Leviticus 11:44-45, 19:2, 21:6, 1 Corinthians 1:2, 1 Peter 1:15, etc...). Christians are often called hypocrites, and in that sense, we often are. If we are to be truthful, we cannot accept the parts of Scripture that we like, and ignore the parts we don't agree with. If God's Word is not *all* true, who will decide which parts of it are lies? God's word is either "the whole Truth," or it is not Truth at all, but the intellectually honest know it must be one way or the other.

Your word, O Lord, is eternal; it stands firm in the heavens.
Psalm 119:89 (NIV)

For ever, O Lord, thy word is settled in heaven.
(KJV)

This is what the Lord says: "Stand in the courtyard of the Lord's house and speak to all the people of the towns of Judah who come to worship in the house of the Lord. Tell them everything I command you; do not omit a word.[3] Perhaps they will listen and each will turn from his evil way. Then I will relent and not bring on them the disaster I was planning because of the evil they have done.[4] Say to them, 'This is what the Lord

Thus saith the Lord; Stand in the court of the Lord's house, and speak unto all the cities of Judah, which come to worship in the Lord's house, all the words that I command thee to speak unto them; diminish not a word: [3] If so be they will hearken, and turn every man from his evil way, that I may repent me of the evil, which I purpose to do unto them because of the evil of their doings. [4] And thou shalt say unto them, Thus saith the

says: If you do not listen to me and follow my law, which I have set before you,[5] and if you do not listen to the words of my servants the prophets, whom I have sent to you again and again (though you have not listened),[6] then I will make this house like Shiloh and this city an object of cursing among all the nations of the earth.'"

Jeremiah 26:2-6 (NIV)

Lord; If ye will not hearken to me, to walk in my law, which I have set before you,[5] To hearken to the words of my servants the prophets, whom I sent unto you, both rising up early, and sending them, but ye have not hearkened;[6] Then will I make this house like Shiloh, and will make this city a curse to all the nations of the earth.

(KJV)

God used the prophet Jeremiah to remind the Israelites of His Law. Jeremiah enraged the crowd when he said God would "make their house like Shiloh," because that meant the people would lose their temple. Losing the temple meant that the religious leaders would lose their power and influence as well, and the thought of that really made them seethe.

Given the situation, it would have been easier for Jeremiah to tell the people what they wanted to hear, but instead, he told them *verbatim* what God said. Jeremiah was only God's messenger, but the people were so angered by what he said that they seized him, shouting that he should be put to death for warning them about the destruction that was sure to come if they didn't change their behavior. Likewise, Jesus enraged people when He told them there would be consequences for their sin (Jeremiah 26:8-11, Matthew 24:2).

Truth always convicts, and conviction always makes sinners uncomfortable. Those who won't accept responsibility for sinful behavior will always attack the messenger because self-indictment is the only other option. But that doesn't mean that Christians should withhold the truth in order to ward off the assault. Quite the contrary. We *must* defend the truth:

So then, brothers, stand firm and hold to the teachings we passed on to you, whether by word of mouth or by letter.

2 Thessalonians 2:15 (NIV)

Therefore, brethren, stand fast, and hold the traditions which ye have been taught, whether by word, or our epistle. **(KJV)**

If there was ever a virtue worth fighting for, it is the virtue of purity. Sexual sin destroys individual lives and families as disease, illegitimacy, divorce and sexual perversions of all kinds are all on the rise because of it. Christians must contend for the faith (Jude 1:3), regardless of how uncomfortable we feel. Whether we are speaking to believers or unbelievers, God intends for *all* Scripture to be passed from generation to generation. Further, the Lord instructs His prophets "not to omit a word." And while it's always more comfortable for us as individuals to ignore sin, doing so never benefits the sinner, nor does it ever glorify God. There will always be those who dilute the Truth in order to accommodate sin, but doing so is always a mistake.

The mourning after

Particularly, when it comes to sexual sin, the after-effects can be so devastating that even the reality of God's unconditional love and forgiveness cannot always stop the pain. In addition to the physical effects (disease or pregnancy), sexual sin typically leaves its prey feeling humiliated, foolish, and remorseful. One can return stolen property or apologize for a wrong done, but one can never recover the irretrievable gift of oneself. Guilt is a spiritually stifling residual effect of sexual sin. Guilt blinds one to God's grace and mercy.

God's forgiveness is the foundation of Christian love, and we are fools if we fail to take hold of it. When God forgives, He forgives eternally and unconditionally; He remembers our sin no more. Guilt is the result of not believing what God says: *as far as the east is from the west, so far has he removed our transgressions from us* (Psalm 103:12).

No one has the power to erase the consequences of sexual sin, but God's Spirit enables us to live victoriously in spite of them. Most importantly, those who truly desire a "transformed life" through Christ, will have the power, through the Holy Spirit, to "go and sin no more." God cares less about yesterday than He does about what we do from this day forward to prove that our repentance is genuine.

Life Application: Chapter 8

Day One:

What is your (*honest*) opinion regarding sex outside of marriage? Give this some serious thought. For example: How has promiscuous sex changed the Christian community? What part has it had in changing the way society views marriage? What effects has it had on traditional families, etc.?

How would you attempt to change the majority's view of sexual promiscuity?

Why do you think sexual sin is so destructive?

1 Corinthians 3:16

1 Corinthians 6:19

Day Two:

Read Ezekiel 5:11. What does God say about those who defile their bodies?

There are Christians who justify sexual promiscuity because Scripture teaches that God forgives every sin. Read and meditate upon 1 Corinthians 6:12-13. Specifically as the verses relate to sexual intimacy, what do you think the Holy Spirit is teaching us?

Now, look at 1 Corinthians 6:15-17. What do you think it means to be "members of Christ himself"?

What does it mean to be "one with the Lord in spirit"?

As "being one" relates to Eros love, what correlation would you make between being one with the Lord and one with your beloved?

Day Three:

Why does God take sexual sin so seriously? (1 Corinthians 6:18-7:11).

Read 1 Corinthians 7:2-9. What is the reason Paul gives for marriage? v.2

What do verses 3-5 say about intimacy in marriage?

What is the only reason Paul gives for depriving one's spouse of sexual relations, and what reason does he then give for coming together? v.5

What does Paul say about singles and widows (or widowers) who cannot control their sexual desires? v.8-9

Day Four:

Why do you think it's so difficult for unmarried people to abstain from sexual intercourse?

What empowers those who want to, to abstain from sin? (1 Thessalonians 1:5).

Why do you think so many marriages lack Eros?

Do you think it's possible to create Eros feelings? Explain your answer.

Day Five:

What must we do in order to have our sins forgiven? (Acts 3:19).

What happens to our sins, following our repentance? What happens to us?

How does God feel about our former sins? (Isaiah 1:18).

What do you think it means, to "reason" about your sins?
What benefit is there in reasoning with God and with others about sin?

Chapter 9

Charity Love

If I give all I possess to the poor and surrender my body to the flames, but have not love, I gain nothing. …And now these three remain: faith, hope and love. But the greatest of these is love.

1 Corinthians 13:3 & 13

"We do not believe Jesus when he says there is more blessedness, more joy, more lasting pleasure in a life devoted to helping others than there is in a life devoted to our material comfort. And therefore the very longing for contentment which ought to drive us to simplicity of life and labors of love contents itself instead with the broken cisterns of prosperity and comfort.

— John Piper

In 1 Corinthians 13:13, the word "love" translates: *Charity.* Charity, Paul says, exceeds all the other graces. It is the virtue we are to "put on" over all the others (Colossians 3:14), because, of all the virtues, charity is what the Lord wants others to see *first* in His children. Charity is predominant over spiritual insight, intellect, social stature, professional position, and physical abilities and attributes. God is glorified most when our gifts are covered by love because, in expressing love, one provides the most appealing imitation of Christ that humans are capable of.

"Charity' is like the maestro in God's orchestra of spiritual gifts; it directs all the accompanying virtues to play harmoniously for the benefit of others, for the glory of God. Charity sanctions and compels every other gift, and means more than simply giving to those in need. Charity exceeds the Christian obligation to address human suffering, and attends to the *motive and quality* of giving. In order for you and me to love as God does, our charity must overflow. Our Lord is not only generous, He is *lavishly* so(1 John 3:1), because of His Agape love for *all* people. When Jesus fed the five thousand, He fed them so abundantly that the disciples needed seven baskets in order to gather what was left! (Matthew 15:36-37).

Quite directly, Paul is saying that charity is meaningless if there is no compassion toward the object of one's gift. Compassion is the ability to show mercy for mercy's sake, to forgive and love others because we understand the meaning of God's grace to *us*; it is a result of one's *choice* to love others.

Charity gains nothing if the heart of the giver isn't first and wholly surrendered to God, and giving because of a desire to share God's love with others. This is precisely why works can't gain salvation (Ephesians 2:8). *Charity is not a means to salvation; it is evidence of the life that has already been transformed by faith.* Charity is but one good *result* of life in Christ. Absent the love of God, and without Christ's compassion to motivate charity, any offering is as filthy rags (Isaiah 64:6).

Many of us serve and give out of obedience and duty. We don't (always) feel love and compassion for the recipient of our generosity, but we want to give because we know that Christ commands it. God gets little glory from loveless deeds (1 Corinthians 13:3).

"I the Lord search the heart and examine the mind, to reward a man according to his conduct, according to what his deeds deserve."
Jeremiah 17:10 (NIV)

I the Lord search the heart, I try the reins, even to give every man according to his ways, and according to the fruit of his doings.
(KJV)

God is most glorified when love is our motive for giving, but that doesn't mean we shouldn't give unless we have a compelling desire to do so. When the primary goal is to imitate Christ, God will grow us through every life experience. Spiritual fruits are like any other; they must mature and ripen on the vine. Obligatory obedience may not be the best motivation for charity, but it is a product beneficial to the cultivation of luscious, sweet spiritual fruits.

Marianna's neighbor (we'll call her Bessie) recently had back surgery. Bessie is a widow, in her mid-seventies. Her only daughter (who works full time) is divorced, has four young children, and lives two thousand miles away; it was impossible for her to help Bessie once she was sent home to recuperate.

"The surgery was a major deal," Marianna says. "The doctor said recovery would take six weeks, and maybe more because of her age. I'm the closest to the situation because she lives next-door, so I agreed to recruit some help for her. When I started phoning the other neighbors, no one wanted to help. Bessie's...well, let's just say she's ornery. Over the years, she's offended almost everyone.

"When I told the neighbors about the painful surgery she's had and how she'd be completely helpless for a couple of weeks, no one cared. One even suggested that the pain would be good for her! No one, *including me,* wanted to sit with Bessie and listen to her curse and complain.

"While she was in the hospital, I prayed about my attitude. The more I prayed, the more sympathetic I felt. Her best friend had recently died, and with her daughter so far away, she had no one. I thought about what that would be like; to live your final years on earth, all alone. Then I began to think of all the things she'd done to alienate people over the years and I thought, *if she had just been nice, her life would be so different now; people would want to help her.* But the fact is, she *wasn't* nice. Bessie had chosen her behavior, and now she was paying the consequences.

"I felt no love for Bessie, but I felt the Holy Spirit leading me to show Christ's love to her. For several days, I cooked for her, cared for her, and listened to her complain. When I asked myself, *Why am I doing this?,* the answer would come: *You're doing it for Me.*

"Bessie's really healthy and she recuperated quickly. She was able to walk after about ten days, so I filled her freezer with individual meals that she could pop in the microwave and told her I wouldn't be coming over as often. I promised to call her every day.

"I stood in Bessie's living room with my hand on the doorknob, waiting for her to thank me for all I'd done. But she never did. Instead, leaning on her walker, she glared at me and said, 'I guess all that Christian mumbo-jumbo paid off. At least you act like one.'

Mariana smiled. "It wasn't much," she said, "...but it was the best Bessie could do. When I told my husband what she'd done, he said, 'She didn't know it, but that's the highest compliment she could give you.' And he's right."

Marianna says that in the weeks following her time with Bessie, God *did* give her love for her neighbor. "It's not the, *I love you and want to be with you* kind of love," she admits. "It's the compassionate kind of love that really cares about her soul, even when she's grouchy. I make it a point to visit Bessie a couple times every month; she's my mission project this year," Marianna says. "Last time, I invited her to church. She said, 'maybe some other time.' But at least she didn't say no!"

When one's motive is pure, God's love will be evident, even when we don't feel it. But if our real motivation is selfish for any reason, nothing is gained for anyone. And in the end, God will reward us according to what the deed deserves.

Charity is the virtue that tells us, *Yes, Bessie's a grouch, but God loves her anyway. And since Jesus isn't her neighbor and I am, I will physically love her for Him.* Our obligation is to determine to love. God's promise is that He will provide compassion where there is none. Once we decide to offer charity for God's sake alone, the Holy Spirit will do the rest.

I will give you a new heart and put a new spirit in you; I will remove from you your heart of stone and give you a heart of flesh.

Ezekiel 36:26 (NIV)

***A new heart also will I give you, and a new spirit will I put within you: and I will take away the stony heart out of your flesh, and I will give you an heart of flesh.* (KJV)**

To think and act toward all humankind as Jesus did, is proof that one's faith has saved him from the world. As with all the other types of love, charity is focused on *others;* it seeks nothing for itself.

Love is patient, love is kind. It does not envy, it does not boast, it is not proud. 5 It is not rude, it is not self-seeking, it is not easily angered, it

Charity suffereth long, and is kind; Charity envieth not; Charity vaunteth not itself, is not puffed up, 5 Doth not behave itself unseemly,

keeps no record of wrongs. [6] Love does not delight in evil but rejoices with the truth. [7] It always protects, always trusts, always hopes, always perseveres.

1 Corinthians 13:4-7 (NIV)

seeketh not her own, is not easily provoked, thinketh no evil; [6] Rejoiceth not in iniquity, but rejoiceth in the truth; [7] Beareth all things, believeth all things, hopeth all things, endureth all things.

(KJV)

The effects of charity are patience, kindness, humility, gentleness, goodness, truth, and hope. Charity, absent of such virtues, is worthless. For example, to pray for a compassionate heart is to ask God to take us beyond our Christian obligation to tend to the physical and spiritual needs of others. It means that we want to understand what the object of our charity feels; we want to discern all that the other requires, so that we can give him *everything* he needs. Then, the act of charity surpasses mere giving and becomes *relational.* Now it's not about what we are doing or giving; it's about the recipient of our gift.

Who cares?

Culturally, we're conditioned to admire those who are smart, attractive, and successful. In the flesh, all of us have felt a pang of jealousy toward another who is better looking or wealthier than we are. Most of us are prone to admire those with academic degrees, prestigious careers, or exceptional talent because we evaluate others for all the wrong reasons. We seldom meet someone for the first time, and wonder how much he loves others. Or if he cares at all about the millions of people who are going through life without Christ. But in fact, that is what God cares about most.

As Christians, we care about people, but when contemplating the issue of Christian charity, we must ask a thoughtful question: *how deeply do we care?*

And this is my prayer: that your love will abound more and more in knowledge and depth of insight,

And this I pray, That your love may abound yet more and more in knowledge and in all judgement

so that you may be able to discern what is best and may be pure and blameless until the day of Christ, filled with the fruit of righteousness that comes through Jesus Christ—to the glory and praise of God. **Philippians 1:9-11 (NIV)**

that ye may approve things that are excellent; that ye may be sincere and without offence till the day of Christ; Being filled with the fruits of righteousness, which are by Jesus Christ, unto the glory and praise of God. **(KJV)**

The "fruit of righteousness" is manifest in Christian charity; it is the rich harvest of our giving to others.

Love serves

Charity is what leads Christians out of the air-conditioned comfort of their living rooms, into the stifling heat of the inner city. It's the virtue that stirs compassion for prisoners, prostitutes, and drug addicts. Charity is the characteristic of love that compels the disciples of Christ to feed the hungry, clothe the naked, and shelter the homeless. Charity is the physical *action* of love. Until Christ returns, Christians must be His heart and hands throughout the world. By using whatever gifts we have to serve others, God's grace is administered through us (1 Peter 4:10).

Saint or sluggard?

Those who just go through the motions of Christian life can find inexhaustible reasons *not* to serve: *I'm not qualified...I may fail... I'm too busy... If I don't do it, someone else will...* For whatever reason, they think that when Jesus said, *"feed my lambs,"* he couldn't have possibly been referring to *them.* Others won't serve unless they're assured the proper recognition or reward; if they agree to give, they must know that they'll get something in return. Jesus speaks of them all in the book of Revelation: *"I know your deeds; you have a reputation of being alive, but you are dead. Wake up! Strengthen what remains and is about to die, for I have not found your deeds complete in the sight of my God' (Revelation 3:1-2).*

Sadly, those who don't serve miss the blessing and spiritual benefit that comes from Christian charity.

God is not unjust; he will not forget your work and the love you have shown him as you have helped his people and continue to help them. [11] We want each of you to show this same diligence to the very end, in order to make your hope sure.

Hebrews 6:10-11 (NIV)

For God is not unrighteous to forget your work and labour of love, which ye have shewed toward his name, in that ye have ministered to the saints, and do minister. [11] And we desire that every one of you do shew the same diligence to the full assurance of hope unto the end:

(KJV)

Service is important because it shifts our focus from *self* to *others.* Paul said, *"I will very gladly spend for you everything I have, and expend myself as well" (2 Corinthians 2:15).* Paul couldn't do enough for God's people. He served tirelessly, under great persecution and without reward, because of his love for God and his gratitude for what God had given him; eternal life through the Son, Jesus Christ: the *indescribable gift.*

This service that you perform is not only supplying the needs of God's people but is also overflowing in many expressions of thanks to God. [13] Because of the service by which you have proved yourselves, men will praise God for the obedience that accompanies your confession of the gospel of Christ, and for your generosity in sharing with them and with everyone else. [14] And in their prayers for you their hearts will go out to you, because of the surpassing grace God has given you. [15] Thanks be to God for his indescribable gift!

2 Corinthians 9:12-15 (NIV)

For the administration of this service not only supplieth the want of the saints, but is abundant also by many thanksgivings unto God; [13] Whiles by the experiment of this ministration they glorify God for your professed subjection into the gospel of Christ, and for your liberal distribution unto them, and unto all men; [14] And by their prayer for you, which long after you for the exceeding grace of God in you. [15] Thanks be unto God for his unspeakable gift. **(KJV)**

Salvation is only the *beginning* of the Christian life. Charity is the means by which believers "work out" their salvation (Philippians 2:12), by offering themselves as "living sacrifices" to be used by God (Romans 12:1). In addition to verbally preaching the Gospel, believers must live it out through acts of Charity.

For a moment, consider the others around you: the friend in need... the co-worker who tells you his problems... the child who is always in trouble... the relative who drinks too much... the grouchy neighbor. Now, consider this: the sovereign hand of God placed each of them within *your* sphere of influence for a reason. *If you want to be like the Shepherd, you must care for your flock.* Every man, woman, and child needs to know Jesus, and *you* may be the closest thing to Jesus that person ever sees. To be a reflection of Christ is an awesome responsibility, and one that God will hold you and me accountable for.

To the elders among you, I appeal as a fellow elder, a witness of Christ's sufferings and one who also will share in the glory to be revealed: [2] Be shepherds of God's flock that is under your care, serving as overseers—not because you must, but because you are willing, as God wants you to be; not greedy for money, but eager to serve; [3] not lording it over those entrusted to you, but being examples to the flock. [4] And when the Chief Shepherd appears, you will receive the crown of glory that will never fade away. **1 Peter 5:1-4 (NIV)**

The elders which are among you I exhort, who am also an elder, and a witness of the sufferings of Christ, and also a partaker of the glory that shall be revealed: [2] Feed the flock of God which is among you, taking the oversight thereof, not by constraint, but willingly; not for filthy lucre, but of a ready mind; [3] Neither as being lords over God's heritage, but being ensamples to the flock. [4] And when the chief Shepherd shall appear, ye shall receive a crown of glory that fadeth not away. **(KJV)**

Not everyone is an "elder" in the literal sense, but every Christian is a "shepherd" to someone. In the Biblical context, a good shepherd is strong, selfless, and devoted to his flock. He provides for, protects, and guides his sheep. He invests enormous time and effort, because he knows that doing so will keep them close to the shepherd. The Lord cares less about the number of sheep we have, than He does about the quality of care we give them (1 John 4:11-12). To ignore another's suffering, is to ignore God's command to bear one another's burdens (Galatians 6:2, Colossians 3:12-14). To know that someone is hungry and not feed him, is to deny another the love of God (1 John 3:17). If you know that someone is troubled or sinning but you fail to provide godly counsel, you may delay or even prevent that person from experiencing victory through Christ (Proverbs 9:9,11:14, 15:22). At its best, charity *seeks* ways to serve.

Life Application: Chapter Nine

Day One:
Read the following verses and record some of the reasons for demonstrating charity:

Hebrews 6:10

2 Corinthians 5:10

James 2:17

John 15:8

Matthew 5:16

Day Two:
Which is harder for you to give, your time or your money? Why?

Do you think giving needs to be sacrificial in order for it to be true charity? Explain.

Note: Hopefully, we understand that charity does not seek it's own reward (Matthew 6:1). The questions below are not intended to inspire pride or guilt; they are simply a means by which to share ideas for Christian service.

What are some ways in which you serve the Body of Christ?

Why is it important to show the love of Christ to unbelievers? (1 Peter 2:12).

What are some ways in which you have demonstrated charity to unbelievers?

On a scale from one to ten, with one being full-time service to others, how would you rate yourself?

1____2____3____4____5___6____7____8____9____10____

How do you *wish* you could rate yourself?

What keeps you from spending more time in service to others?

Day Three:

Read 2 Corinthians 8:12 and explain why the willing servant of God need never fear failure.

Read Colossians 3:23-24. How are we instructed to serve God?

When the motivation for service is to demonstrate love for God, there is always a reward. What is it? (v. 24)

What should prompt us to serve others? (1 Thessalonians 1:3).

What should inspire us to persevere in service?

Day Four:
The following questions are designed to stimulate you to use your gifts to help others. Please think carefully, evaluate yourself honestly, and record everything that comes to mind:

What types of service bring you the most joy?

What special gifts has God given you?

List some ways that you can use your gifts to help others:

Day Five:
Read Matthew 25:40-46 and answer the following questions:
When you serve, who is actually the recipient of your charity?

To whom is Jesus speaking in verses 42 & 43?

Why do you think so many Christians fail to show charity to others?

Why is charity such an important part of the Christian life?

Read Ecclesiastes 12:14 and record what it says:

In the space below, list one thing you plan to do to show charity to another this week:

Chapter 10

Love of the World

Do not love the world or anything in the world. If anyone loves the world, the love of the Father is not in him. For everything in the world—the cravings of sinful man, the lust of his eyes and the boasting of what he has and does—comes not from the Father but from the world. The world and its desires pass away, but the man who does the will of God lives forever.

1 John 2:15-17 (NIV)

Since all wars and fightings come from the corruptions of our own hearts, it is right to mortify those lusts that war in the members. Wordly and fleshly lusts are distempers, which will not allow content or satisfaction. Sinful desires and affections stop prayer, and the working of our desires toward God.

— Matthew Henry

Within the context of Scripture, the word *world* is often used symbolically, referring to anything that directs the human heart away from God. Worldliness, or "love of the world" is an *attitude* that affects our choices. "World*view*" is about priorities; it defines what's most important to us. Worldview determines how we think about others, what kind of friends we choose, and what we do with our spare time. It also determines how we spend money, how much value we place on material possessions, and how we view personal power. Most importantly, one's worldview determines the way in which he sees and defines God.

Scripture is the singular foundation for a "biblical" or "godly" worldview. Conversely, a "worldly" or "carnal" worldview results from any number (or combination of) humanly devised philosophies or value systems. When one claims a biblical worldview, he maintains that God's Word is the standard by which he strives to live. He attempts to understand the world through God's eyes, and to react to life circumstances in ways that glorify God. For example, when he sees sin in the culture, he speaks out against it; he knows that sin grieves our Holy God, so he makes the case for righteous living. And when it comes to money, material possessions, or power, the godly man views all as temporal gifts from God. He is not the "owner" of what he has; he is the "steward" of what belongs to God. He enjoys the things of the world, but he lives for the Giver. He doesn't boast of what he has or does, he delights in acknowledging and praising God for it. By way of contrast, two words will precisely define "worldly" love: selfish desire.

Worldliness is about what we long for, in relation to carnal pleasures. Like all desires, love of the world begins in the heart. Since all are born with "hard" hearts, separated from God by sin (Ephesians 4:17-18), we all struggle with worldly desires to some degree. So, love of the world is an *ex*ternal, as well as an internal, problem.

Internally, worldliness has devastating spiritual effects. In a few words, those who invest in *this* world will lose everything in the next. In the end, all that worldly men and women worked for will go up in flames (Revelation18:9-10, 2 Peter 3:7). Only faith, hope, and love will remain because, while *the world always fails*, love *never* fails. It is an absolute fact that those who put their hope and trust in the world will be destroyed, but those whose hope and faith are in the Lord will live forever. God offers us eternal life, while Satan offers us the world (Matthew 4:8-10). Sadly, many opt for what can be immediately seen because the god of this world blinds them from what can be realized.

..."No eye has seen, no ear has heard, no mind has conceived what God has prepared for those who love him."
1 Corinthians 2:9 (NIV)

But as it is written, Eye hath not seen, nor ear heard, neither have entered into the heart of man, the things which God hath prepared for them that love him. **(KJV)**

Some think it unfair that God puts us in this awesome world, and then expects us to resist its attractions. But that's exactly what He does. The world, with all its temptations, is the proving ground for God's people. Our faith is confirmed through testing, and no one, not even Jesus Christ, is exempt from it (Matthew 4:1-11). For most of us, it's a tremendous challenge to enter the human race, and run its full course, resisting the temptations of the world. But if we have truly *died with Christ* to the basic principles of this world (Colossians 2:20), the Holy Spirit will empower us to finish well.

Dear friends, I urge you, as aliens and strangers in the world, to abstain from sinful desires, which war against your soul. [12] Live such good lives among the pagans that, though they accuse you of doing wrong, they may see your good deeds and glorify God on the day he visits us. **1 Peter 2:11-12 (NIV)**

Dearly beloved, I beseech you as strangers and pilgrims, abstain from fleshly lusts, which war against the soul; [12] Having your conversation honest among the Gentiles: that, whereas they speak against you as evildoers, they may by your good works, which they shall behold, glorify God in the day of visitation. **(KJV)**

You, dear children, are from God and have overcome them, because the one who is in you is greater than the one who is in the world.
1 John 4:4 (NIV)

Ye are of God, little children, and have overcome them: because greater is he that is in you, than he that is in the world. **(KJV)**

A reality of this world is that Satan exists, and he is everywhere on earth in the form of fleshly pleasures. The desire for money, material possessions, pleasure, illicit entertainment, gambling, personal power, and self-gratification are just some of the things the world offers in hope of pulling us away from God. Satan leads the whole world astray, and as long as God allows, *all of it* is under his control (Revelation 12:9, 1John 5:9). As we near the end times, more and more people will follow after the evil one. Satan is the great deceiver. He makes the most repulsive sins appear attractive, and he has the power to persuade multitudes to accept diabolical evil. Christians must be ever vigilant to protect themselves against love of the world; that affection is a destroyer of souls.

According to 1 John 2:15-16, worldliness is characterized by three attitudes: (1) *the cravings of sinful man* (2) *the lust of his eyes*, and (3) *boasting of what he has and does.* The fact that liberal theologians dilute this passage (by giving it limits and exceptions) does not make the passage any less true. For example, the "believe-it-and-receive-it" preachers teach that there's nothing wrong with craving worldly goods. After all (they claim), God created all things for man to enjoy. Therefore, He will give us any material thing we ask for, if we just "have faith" enough that He will. Others encourage their flocks to "be tolerant" of all types of sexual sin (and even abortion) simply because the world sanctions those sins. And while this makes preaching easy for the one who simply wants to "tickle the ears," such preaching is spiritually deadly and diminishes Christ's death on the cross. He did not die so that we could go on sinning. He died in order to give us the resurrection power necessary to resist it. Those who profess to live under the Lordship of Jesus Christ, cannot afford to miss the real meaning and intent of 1 John 2:15-16. Instead, we must be determined to live holy and obedient lives, in spite of what everyone else is doing.

The cravings of sinful man, the lust of his eyes…

Satan's purpose is to counterfeit or destroy all that is good. To that end, he tempts some to crave sin, they think they must have it. Satan makes sin so attractive that some actually believe there is no quality of life without it, they must have their drug, their sex, their shopping cart, or their power in order to feel "full." In fact, God has already given every believer all that he needs for life *and* godliness (2Peter 1:3), the Spirit of Christ *in* us, fills us (Ephesians 1:22-23, 1 Corinthians 2:12). Satan holds sin out as an offering: *take this,* he says, *and you will be full; this will make you happy.* Christians don't need what the world offers in order to feel joy. Some of us only think we do.

God's Word tells us to *fix our eyes on Jesus (Hebrews 12:2),* but lustful eyes are fixed on the things of the world. Remember, Satan's purpose is to draw all people away from God, so he makes the world as tantalizing as possible. Everywhere God's people look, we see things designed to shift our focus away from holy living. When we consider the sins of the world (sexual sin, murder, pornography, addictions, etc.), the sin of materialism doesn't sound at all shocking. Coveting is such a common sin, that most Christians seldom think about it. But the desire for what we don't have robs us of peace and distracts us from better spiritual pursuits. The one thinking about the new car or the bigger home, is not praising God for what he has... the one consumed with desire for a career promotion may sin or compromise his Christian values in order to get it... the young woman who wants to look like the model in a magazine may abuse her own body in order to get "the look."

To *covet* means to enviously long for something you do not have. One who is covetous, has an excessive desire for wealth, possessions, position, or power. Advertising executives are handsomely compensated for luring you and me to desire and ultimately *buy* what the world has to sell. We lust after luxuries that (we think) will improve our status or make us more comfortable. Or we lust after the job that will create the wealth necessary to have the luxuries. And while it may be a stretch to suggest that some women lust after beauty, vanity keeps a multi-billion dollar cosmetics industry flourishing. Whether or not we admit it, most of us, at some point, have lusted after something other than God. Whatever the object of one's lust, the focus has shifted away from God and onto worldly things.

"Roger" has been a Christian all of his adult life. He attends church every Sunday, and even leads a men's Bible study. The men Roger teaches admire him greatly. He's active in his church and community, and he owns a successful business. In fact, Roger brings home more money in one year than most of us earn in a decade. To most, Roger is the epitome of success. In addition to being rich and successful, his wife is beautiful, his daughter is a top-seeded junior tennis player, and his son makes the honor role every semester.

One might look at Roger's beautiful home, designer suits, or luxury cars and think, *this is a Christian addicted to material possessions,* but that's not the case. He doesn't care about material things. Instead, Roger cares about the way in which others respond to the things he has; it's praise and recognition that Roger craves. He insists that nothing is worth doing, unless it's done so well that others recognize the achievement and praise the effort. The "things" that Roger possesses are a means to an end; they provide visible proof to others that he has done well.

In the years that I've known Roger, I've learned several things that may contribute to his perceived need for praise and recognition. Most significantly, he was the middle child in a family of seven children, and he has said that he always felt ignored. Secondly, he had a demanding father whom he could never please. Roger only remembers one time that his father acknowledged him for anything. The day Roger announced that he had received an academic scholarship to college, his father said, "*Good job, son.*"

From Roger's perspective, the world's approval is all that matters. He drives his family so hard, that he has alienated all of them. In addition to being so demanding, he has trouble controlling his temper when things don't go the way he'd like. Roger's wife ("Nancy") is so nervous that she bites her nails to the quick. Roger explodes in angry tirades when one of them fails, and she fears his rebukes, especially toward her impressionable teenaged children. And when Nancy tries talking to Roger about the pressure he puts on them, he always dismisses her concern, justifying his behavior instead.

"Roger thinks Melanie excels at tennis because he (*his* words) insists on excellence," Nancy says, "...but she's really motivated by the fact that she wants to travel so she doesn't have to be around him. A few months ago, I found some tranquilizers in her bathroom. She had asked a friend for them because Roger had her so tense about her need to win an upcoming tournament, that she couldn't sleep nights.

"And Roger's fighting with our son right now, because Todd doesn't want him to coach his baseball team. In fact, Todd is so insistent that he says if his dad coaches, he won't play. That's because, when Todd doesn't perform the way Roger thinks he should, Roger berates and humiliates him in front of the other kids. He actually believes that kind of abuse will make Todd try harder.

"I'm not exempt from his disappointment, either," Nancy says. "A few months ago he badgered me into chairing a charity event for one of his favorite causes. I didn't want to do it, but I was trying to please him, so I agreed. I did everything possible to make the event successful; I worked myself to exhaustion for seven months. But when the event was over, we fell almost $3,000 short of what they made last year. I *still* haven't heard the end of that! The way Roger sees it, when one of us fails, *he* fails. And nothing is more important to Roger than how the world views him."

No one escapes this life without adversity. In Roger's case, it's unfortunate that he felt ignored and unappreciated as a child, but he is no longer a child. Roger is a grown man with enough knowledge of Scripture to teach Bible studies. But if he doesn't learn to apply what he knows to his life, God's Word is of no benefit to him. As a child of the Living God, Roger does not need the world's approval. The One who created everything already approves him. From the moment that Roger submitted his life to Christ, the King of Kings loved him deeply and unconditionally. Roger never needed, nor does he now need, to perform.

For it is by grace you have been saved, through faith—and this not from yourselves, it is the gift of God. **Ephesians 2:8 (NIV)**

For by grace are ye saved through faith; and that not of yourselves: it is the gift of God: **(KJV)**

I have no doubt that Roger has saving faith, but like the rest of us, he is still "working out" his salvation. Love is a fruit of the Spirit that has not yet ripened in Roger's life, because if he knew how to love others as Jesus loves him, Roger would care more about his family than he cares about how the world sees them.

Boasting

Roger exemplifies one who is clearly obsessed with his own importance. And while he doesn't always boast verbally, all that Roger does is motivated by his desire to be praised by the world. Instead of giving God glory by acknowledging all He allows by virtue of His grace, Roger draws attention to himself. Clearly, the world admires appearances, but God cares only about the quality of our worship and the diligence with which we seek to know and obey Him.

This is what the Lord says: "Let not the wise man boast of his wisdom or the strong man boast of his strength or the rich man boast of his riches, [24] but let him who boasts boast about this: that he understands and knows me, that I am the Lord, who exercises kindness, justice and righteousness on earth, for in these I delight," declares the Lord. **Jeremiah 9:23-24 (NIV)**

Thus saith the Lord, Let not the wise man glory in his wisdom, neither let the mighty man glory in his might, let not the rich man glory in his riches: [24] But let him that glorieth glory in this, that he understandeth and knoweth me, that I am the Lord which exercise lovingkindness, judgment, and righteousness, in the earth: for in these things I delight, saith the Lord. **(KJV)**

Certain things are true of all who boast: No one does anything apart from God's will to allow him. God owns and gives everything, and if He wills, He can take everything from us in the time that it takes you or me to blink an eye. The Lord destroys the proud, and rewards the humble. God places such value on humility that the Apostle Paul linked the arrogant and boastful with slanderers, and insolent God-haters who invent ways of doing evil. Paul longed to boast of nothing but Christ crucified; his desire was to die to his former love of the world (Romans 1:30, Galatians 6:14). If Roger would likewise put to death his desire for the world's approval, he would understand the importance of living out his faith by loving others with the compassionate and unconditional love of Christ.

Now this is our boast: Our conscience testifies that we have conducted ourselves in the world, and especially in our relations with you, in the holiness and sincerity that are from God. We have done so not according to worldly wisdom but according to God's grace.
2 Corinthians 1:12 (NIV)

For our rejoicing is this, the testimony of our conscience, that in simplicity and godly sincerity, not with fleshly wisdom, but by the grace of God, we have had our conversation in the world, and more abundantly to you-ward. **(KJV)**

A hollow and deceptive philosophy

Love of the world lures Christians away from the light of God's Truth, into the dark abyss of moral relativism. The world entices God's people to desire possessions and status so badly that we are willing to break or compromise God's Law in order to get what we want. And since many have bought the lie that "there is no such thing as absolute truth," God's Truth is now so blurred that many are unable to identify it. Two obvious examples would be cheating and lying in business. I know Christians who don't think twice about "borrowing" supplies from the office, or "shading the truth a bit" in order to gain clientele or cover an honest mistake. And while neither moral failure will rock the world, both are sins, and both are done in plain view of a holy God.

The world tempts us to desire what is sinful, and to take credit for what God has done. We're conditioned to want more than we need, and to want it for the wrong reasons. (It's not *money* that's the "root of all evil;" it's the *love* of money.) And when we get what we want, we boast that it's all the result of our own skill and hard work. Love of the world results in the kind of idolatry that entices Christians to worship material things, and to abandon the pursuit of holiness in favor of running with the pack. The only way to avoid such heresy is to "fix our eyes on Jesus." We must study and obey the Word of God because, in order to resist sin, we must be able to recognize it wherever it appears, and however it disguises itself.

Worldliness is an inferior characteristic that keeps Christians focused on all the wrong things. Human ideas and experiences must never take precedence over truth, and worldly desires must never become more important than heavenly pursuits. Love of the world will only destroy those who pursue it.

See to it that no one takes you captive through hollow and deceptive philosophy, which depends on human tradition and the basic principles of this world rather than on Christ. **Colossians 2:8 (NIV)**

Beware lest any man spoil you through philosophy and vain deceit, after the tradition of men, after the rudiments of the world, and not after Christ. **(KJV)**

Command those who are rich in this present world not to be arrogant nor to put their hope in wealth, which is so uncertain, but to put their hope in God, who richly provides us with everything for our enjoyment. [18] Command them to do good, to be rich in good deeds, and to be generous and willing to share. [19] In this way they will lay up treasure for themselves as a firm foundation for the coming age, so that they may take hold of the life that is truly life.
1 Tim. 6:17-19 (NIV)

Charge them that are rich in this world, that they be not highminded, nor trust in uncertain riches, but in the living God, who giveth us richly all things to enjoy; [18] That they do good, that they be rich in good works, ready to distribute, willing to communicate; [19] Laying up in store for themselves a good foundation against the time to come, that they may lay hold on eternal life. **(KJV)**

To be sure, Jesus sends disciples into the world, but at the same time, He tells us not to love it (John 17:18, 1 John 2:15-16). Everything Jesus taught, contradicts what the world does (Matthew 5:3-5). The abundant life that Jesus came to give does not come through human effort; it is a gift of God to all who honor Him through faith and obedience.

Life Application: Chapter 10

Day One:

How did Noah prove his faith? (Hebrews 11:7).

What did Noah gain by condemning the world?

Read and meditate upon Psalm 49:16-17. In the space below, record all of your insights into the verses:

Why is there nothing to be gained from desiring the world? (Haggai 1:6).

Do you think it's possible for man to ever be completely satisfied? Explain your answer.

Day Two:

How would you describe the "way of the world"? (Proverbs 14:12 , NIV).

Why do you think so many Christians want what the world wants? Think carefully and record every answer you can think of.

Read 1 Timothy 6:7. What do you think about the pursuit of "things?"

What material possession are you most attached to?

What do you think is the worst thing that could happen if you lost that possession and had no means to get it back?

What does God say about Christians who "love to party" with the world? (Proverbs 23:20-21).

Day Three:

Read Ecclesiastes 2:3-11 and make a list of everything Solomon did to create pleasure for himself:

What did Solomon deny himself? v.10

What was the end result of Solomon's labors? v.11

In what ways do you identify with Solomon?

Considering all that God has made, what is the most beautiful vision you have seen on earth?

Read 1 Corinthians 2:9. In what ways do you think the beauty of Heaven will differ from beauty here on earth?

Read Ecclesiastes 11:9 and paraphrase what it says. What do you think of Solomon's advice?

Would you give your own child this same advice? Explain your answer.

Day Four:

Read Ephesians 2:1-5. How does Scripture define those who follow the ways of the world? vs. 1 & 3

List some ways in which Christians seek to "gratify the cravings of their sinful nature"

Who controls those who live for the world? v.2

Day Five:
How does one escape the corruption of the world? (2 Peter 2:20).

What does Peter say about Christians who love the world?

What do you think it means when he says they "are worse off at the end?" Compare with Matthew 7:20-23.

What gives you the power to change your behavior? (1 John 5:4-5).

What does it mean, to "overcome the world"?

What "worldly" behaviors do you have that you'd like to change?

What steps do you plan to take in order to change your worldly behavior?

Keep on loving each other as brothers. Do not forget to entertain strangers, for by so doing some people have entertained angels without knowing it. Remember those in prison as if you were their fellow prisoners, and those who are mistreated as if you yourselves were suffering. Marriage should be honored by all, and the marriage bed kept pure, for God will judge the adulterer and all the sexually immoral. Keep your lives free from the love of money and be content with what you have, because God has said, "Never will I leave you; never will I forsake you."

Hebrews 13:1-5 (NIV)

Other Books in this Series

The Fruit of the Spirit is....Peace
The Fruit of the Spirit is....Patience
The Fruit of the Spirit is....Self-Control

Lynn Stanley is available to speak at conferences.
To contact Lynn, or for comments on this study or information regarding other studies in this series,
please visit **www.focus publishing.com**